EXTRA TIME AND IT'S STILL A FUNNY OLD GAME

EXTRA TIME AND IT'S STILL A FUNNY OLD GAME

Ian St John and Jimmy Greaves
Edited by Bob Patience

Illustrations by Robin Bouttell

Stanley Paul
London : Sydney : Auckland : Johannesburg

Stanley Paul and Co Ltd

An imprint of Century Hutchinson

Brookmount House, 62-65 Chandos Place,
Covent Garden, London WC2N 4NW

Century Hutchinson Australia (Pty) Ltd
20 Alfred Street, Milsons Point, Sydney 2061, Australia

Century Hutchinson New Zealand Limited
191 Archers Road, PO Box 40-086, Glenfield, Auckland 10

Century Hutchinson South Africa (Pty) Ltd
PO Box 337, Bergvlei 2012, South Africa

First published in 1989

Printed and bound in Great Britain by Scotprint,
Musselburgh

British Library Cataloguing in Publication Data
St. John, Ian
   It's a funny old game: according to Saint and Greavsie.
   1. Association football
   I. Title II. Greaves, James, 1940-
   796.334

ISBN 0 09 174251 X

Photograph acknowledgements

The authors and publishers would like to thank the
following for allowing use of copyright photographs:

AllSport: Ronnie Whelan, p.6 (photo by Simon Bruty);
Roy Aitken, p.6 (photo by David Cannon); George
Graham, p.6; Terry Butcher, p.6 (photo by Ben Radford);
FA Cup Final, p.9 (two pictures); Rangers, p.11 (two
pictures by Ben Radford); John Charles, p.40; Neville
Southall, p.47; Bob Paisley, p.54; FA Cup Final, p.66
(three pictures by Simon Bruty and Pascale Rondeau);
Chris Woods, p.67 (photo by David Cannon); Peter
Shreeves, p.88; Trevor Putney, p.101; Jock Stein, p.107;
Jock Wallace, p.115; Ally McCoist, p.120
Colorsport: Ian St John, p.7; Ian McColl, p.10; John
White, p.13; Jim Baxter, p.14; Jimmy Johnstone, p.18;
Peter and John Sillett, p.20; Dennis Evans, p.21; Alan
Mullery, p.22; Bobby Moore, p.24; Paul Gascoigne, p.26;
Denis Law, p.26; Terry Venables and Terry Mancini, p.27;
Ian Storey-Moore, p.28; Brian Clough, p.29; Keith
Newton, p.31; Bill Shankly, p.34; Tommy Younger, p.45;
Albert Iremonger, p.49; Stan Mortensen, p.57; George
Young, p.59; Jim Baxter, p.14; Danny Blanchflower and Stanley Matthews,
p.63; Scottish Cup Final, p.67 (two pictures); Jack
Charlton, p.73; Don Revie, p.78; George Mulhall, p.79;
Alan Waddle, p.81; Tommy Docherty, p.83; Rodney
Marsh, p.85; Ted Drake, p.87; Malcolm Allison, p.90; Billy
Bingham, p.91; Stan Cullis, p.93; Sir Alf Ramsey, p.99;
Jim Craig, p.105; Tommy Gemmell, p.109; Bobby
Murdoch, p.109; Bobby Lennox, Colin Jackson and John
Greig, p.112; Derek Johnstone, p.114; Tom Forsyth, p.117;
Ally MacLeod, p.121
Sport and General: Billy Bremner and Les Cocker, p.35;
Tom Finney, p.54/55; Malcolm Macdonald, p.85
Bob Thomas: Paddy Crerand and Jim Baxter, p.16; Jack
Charlton and Bobby Robson, p.23; Kenny Dalglish, p.25;
Brian Clough, p.37; Peter Shilton, p.43; Pat Jennings and
Ray Clemence, p.46; Bobby Robson, p.95; Allan Hunter,
p.96; Mich d'Avray, p.101

And special thanks are due to Barry Roberts for his two
cartoons.

CONTENTS

The joy of winning
Ronnie Whelan lifts the FA Cup for Liverpool, Roy
Aitken the Scottish Cup for Celtic, George Graham
the League trophy for Arsenal, and Terry Butcher
the Premier League trophy for Rangers

SAINT
1 A TOUCH OF THE INTERNATIONALS

Ian St John may be known nowadays as one of the top sporting personalities on British television, but of course Ian was an outstanding centre-forward with Liverpool in the great days of Bill Shankly, and he was also a much feared and respected striker in one of Scotland's best-ever international teams during the sixties. In his international capacity, Ian played with and against some of the biggest names of the day. In this chapter, he remembers some of the greats, both on and off the park, with a selection of hilarious anecdotes of just what happens behind the scenes in international football.

My international career spanned six years between 1959 and 1965. During that period I attended no World Cup Finals, no European Cup Finals and lost 9–3 to England. But the 21 caps that I gathered represent 21 of the proudest and most exciting days of my life.

To walk out onto Hampden Park in the days when 100,000 was a disappointing crowd was an experience like no other. Just recalling the feeling sends a shiver down my spine – goodness only knows what it did to the opposition.

The Hampden Roar is legendary. Not a chant or an anthem, just a gathering crescendo of noise that you think cannot get any louder, but grows and grows until your eardrums are ringing and your heart is pounding. If you think it is deafening up there on the open terraces, you should hear it swirling around down at pitch level. I've never heard anything so inspiring.

The Saint demonstrates the classic double-footed kick which he perfected whilst playing for Scotland

I owe my international breakthrough and my first taste of the Hampden experience to the highly organised state of Scottish football in 1959. I was down to play for the Under-23 team, but when the seniors' centre-forward Andy Kerr got injured in training there was nobody else around!

The manager in those days had as much say in the selection of the Scotland team as my wife has today! It was none of his business who played. Such matters could not be entrusted to people like Andy Beattie or Matt Busby. Teams were selected by committee, and the representatives of Brechin City and Montrose would have as much say in the matter as those from Celtic and Rangers. It was like the House of Lords telling Kenny Dalglish who to pick for Liverpool!

Mind you, I shouldn't complain too much because there was a Motherwell director, Mr Hepburn, on the selection committee. So there were three of us in the side to take on West Germany that night – Bert McCann, Andy Weir and me. I'd been running my socks off in a training session with the Under-23s up at Turnberry when I was called over and told I was going to play for the big boys. I thought to myself: 'I'll be knackered.'

We beat a team including Seeler and Schnellinger and Rahn by three goals to two. John White – the late, great Tottenham inside-forward – made his debut alongside me. I laid on a goal for him, and the morning headlines read: 'St John and White make the future look bright'. I didn't play again for five months!

I was chosen for the first international of the following season, a 4–0 win in Belfast which I recall for one of the strangest penalties I've ever seen. It was awarded to Northern Ireland and taken by Burnley's Jimmy McIlroy. He walked up to place the ball on the spot and took the kick while he was bending down to position it. Bill Brown, our keeper, was going through his usual routine, banging his gloves together and looking at the two posts to make sure he was in the centre of his goal. He never even saw Jimmy take it. He looked at him as if to say, 'Okay, I'm ready. Get on with it.' The ball had already rolled past the post and away for a goal-kick. Everyone was taken by surprise – not least Jimmy!

I got my first goal against Poland in the May. It was rather overshadowed by one of the greatest goals I've ever witnessed by their left-winger – an angled shot from thirty yards which found the top corner of those king-sized Hampden goals. But I thought I had seen everything by then because I had already played my first game against England.

Like the first hiding you take from your dad and your very first kiss, your first England international is a case of 'close your eyes and hope for the best'. Jet engines and television cameras have caused the world to shrink and opened our eyes to the glamour of World Cups and the like during the last twenty years, but in those days the only international that mattered was the England match. It was the World Cup and the World War rolled into one.

Actually, I contrived to miss a great match-winning chance in that first England game at Hampden in 1960, but it passed by almost unnoticed in the mayhem of the occasion. Team talks before taking on England were dismissive. Banks? – rubbish! . . . Moore? – he panics! . . . Haynes? – no class! I remember our earnest full-back Alec Hamilton confidently assuring us all that he'd have Bobby Charlton tucked away in his back-pocket by five past three. Bobby had probably never even heard of Alec, but we were filled with blind faith before we went out. 'Any questions?' . . . 'No, right, let's give them what for.' End of team talk.

Ian McColl was our manager for a spell, and I'll never forget his talk before a game against foreign opposition at Hampden. He

Michael Thomas scores the last ditch winner for Arsenal against Liverpool to clinch not only the game but also the league title, in the nail-biting climax to the 1988/89 season

Ian McColl, former Scotland manager, who warned of the opposition's 'bolt system'!

warned us that they might use the 'bolt system'. None of us had a clue what he was talking about, and Denis Law and Jim Baxter were giggling away in the corner with the rest of us trying desperately not to laugh too. I still don't know to this day whether or not they used the 'bolt system', but we beat them all the same. We convinced ourselves we could conquer the world.

Our world fell out of the London sky briefly on 15 April, 1961. It was my first international for nearly a year . . . since a 4–1 defeat in Vienna when we had been exposed as a stone-age force in tactical terms. That was heaven compared with what was to follow.

Frank Haffey was our goalkeeper on that fateful day at Wembley. He was our third choice – honest! – Bill Brown and Lawrie Leslie were injured. Frank had made his reputation within the squad as a good singer. It turned out that he was a much better singer than he was a goalkeeper. Everything they seemed to hit at him went in. We lost 9–3.

Later that night a few of us were walking along Shaftesbury Avenue looking for somewhere to drown our sorrows when we were spotted by some Scottish fans whose loyalty had taken a bit of a pounding. We ran after the nearest bus and jumped on. Frank just made it to the accompaniment of 'that's the first thing you've caught today, Haffey'. Good judges, Scottish fans. He emigrated to Australia eventually, but they'll catch up with him one day.

In Scotland, Rangers may have lost the last league game of the season (3–0 to Aberdeen) but they comfortably won the Premier League

It was the one England international that I played in where there was a trophy for the winners. It suddenly appeared when we were at our lowest ebb, and we all had to troop up the steps and shake hands and smile at the Queen. It's the closest you've ever been to a revolution, Your Majesty.

Bobby Robson took the stick on everyone else's behalf . . . as usual. Denis Law made a mess of his leg with one rather rash challenge. I can still see poor Bobby looking up at Denis as if to say, 'Why me?' . . . and Denis looking down at him as if to say, 'Be careful, or I'll give you another leg to match'. We weren't exactly world-class losers.

The names of both Law and St John failed to appear on the team-sheet for the next Scottish match. In the best traditions of the national selection committee, the two full-backs and the centre-half were retained, whilst the forwards were dropped.

Just before the 9–3 game all of us had been asked to fill in visa application forms for a forthcoming trip to Czechoslovakia. In the early hours of that Sunday morning I sat with my Motherwell team-mates Pat Quinn and Bert McCann debating whether to complete the form or set fire to it. Bert and I burnt ours, Pat held on to his. He was chosen, we weren't. Call it a footballer's instinct!

I waited another five months for my next cap by which time my favourite forward-line was beginning to take shape. It was September 1961 and I was recalled to partner Denis Law and John White. Davie Wilson was already installed on the left-wing, Willie Henderson would arrive shortly on the right. Give me Paddy Crerand and Jim Baxter and a sound defence and I'll take on your all-stars' selection tomorrow with that Scottish team.

Wee Willie was the classic Scottish winger who could disappear with a ball for a year before anybody would get it off him. Oddly enough, he was terribly short-sighted. I'll never forget the groundsman at Ibrox asking him whether he wanted the lines painting brighter or kerbs building instead. Contact lenses probably saved his career. You could call him and he'd ask you who it was. But put a ball at his feet and he could see all he needed to. He was a great gambler, too. He'd bet on his ability at snooker, putting, anything. Baxter used to take him to the cleaners!

Davie Wilson was a lovely, happy-go-lucky type. He had the pace and could cut in and score you a goal. We all thought he dyed his hair blonde and used to rib him unmercifully. But I saw him recently and he's got more on top than the rest of us put together, so he's had the last laugh.

John White was a practical joker. I remember seeing him in a black polo-neck sweater before dinner one night, and when he came into the dining room, he'd attached white cloth around the neck and pinched the Bible out of his room and spent the meal impersonating a vicar.

They called him 'The Ghost' because of his ability to drift around the field into telling positions. Alf Ramsey said Martin Peters was ten years ahead of his time; well, John was twenty. He could pass a ball from here to John O'Groats and run twice as far again.

You were never safe when he was around. When you were given tickets to leave at the ground for your family, Whitey would pinch them and tear them up into confetti, and put them back in the envelope. Dave Mackay tricked him one day, and pinched John's. Whitey thought he was stealing Dave's tickets and promptly tore up his own.

I'll never forget the day he died. I was very ill in hospital with a collapsed appendix. The news of his passing very nearly finished me off.

John 'The Ghost' White, practical joker

The Lawman was different again. We came through the Under-23s together. He was never the greatest trainer in the world, always had a strain or a twinge which made him a doubt until it was match-day. But you could forgive him when you saw the energy and the commitment he gave to the game. He and I were two of the five survivors of the 9–3 match who played in the revenge game against England at Hampden in 1962. We won 2–0, our first victory over the old enemy at Hampden since the War, and the crowd called us out for a lap of honour.

A year later and, sweeter still, victory at Wembley. It was a victory won by only ten men. Eric Caldow broke his leg in a first-half clash with Bobby Smith, but we came through 2–1. Slim Jim Baxter was the hero, but wasn't he always?

When a vital penalty needed taking that day we all looked around for a volunteer. There was nothing so organised as appointed penalty-takers in those days, but Jim was *self*-appointed. 'I'll take it,' he said and stroked it in. He got the winner too. He could have moved to Edinburgh Castle if he had wanted to that night.

Scotland has never had a bigger hero than Slim Jim. When Baxter sneezed, the whole of the country shouted 'bless you' in unison. We once played an international in Norway and Jim left his boots behind at Ibrox. The evening newspaper carried the headline, 'Baxter arrives without boots'. It was a state of emergency. The boots were sent by express courier to the main man in Oslo. The nation breathed a collective sigh of relief.

He was our George Best. As a player he had ability to spare and twice as much confidence again. Like many of the world's great left-footers – Puskas, Maradona and so on – he had an extra helping of star quality. Jim Baxter lived his life in the same lane as George Best too. His on-the-field arrogance enabled him to take control of a game, but when it spilled over into his social life it led him into games he couldn't control. For somebody who couldn't fight to save his life, he always seemed to be getting into one.

Alex Young told me a story about an argument he had with Jim during an after-match celebration. Jim challenged Alex to step outside and resolve their differences in the street. Youngy hadn't been in a scrap since his schooldays, but couldn't say no. They squared up in the street and Alex threw the first punch. Jim took it, shook Youngy's hand and said, 'that'll do, let's go back inside'! He was never a fighting man.

Denis Law once scored four times in a game against Northern Ireland in Belfast where Billy Bingham took us to a party at the late Alex Harvey's house. The party was in full swing when Jim arrived, hit the Lawman in the eye, then left. Denis being Denis just shrugged his shoulders and forgot about it. Baxter was lucky it hadn't happened in a game. Denis was less forgiving on the field.

But Jim could look after himself in the middle, with a little help from his mates like John Greig and Paddy Crerand. At Wembley in 1967 he tormented England's World Cup-winning team with a performance still talked about in Scotland. He ran the show from beginning to end, putting his foot on the ball and taunting little Alan Ball. 'Do you want it, son? Well, come and get it,' he was saying as Bally chased around after him. Greavsie played that day so I suppose it wasn't the real England World Cup team!

We had some outstanding wing-halves in those days . . . what with Baxter and Crerand and Dave Mackay and Frank McLintock and Billy Bremner and Jimmy Gabriel all fight-

When 'Slim' Jim Baxter sneezed, the whole of Scotland shouted 'Bless you' in unison

Paddy Crerand and Jim Baxter had a wet sponge fight!

ing over a couple of places. It was some fight as you can imagine!

I remember us playing Czechoslovakia in a play-off game for World Cup qualification in Brussels in 1961, and Crerand and Baxter started fighting each other. One of them had the trainer's sponge, and the other one wanted it. They ended up scuffling over a wet sponge in the middle of a World Cup decider. Some of the other lads jumped into part them, and I recall yelling out, 'Let's fight THEM if we're going to fight anybody.' Isn't it strange how Scots have a habit of reaching for the self-destruct button?

We were one game away from reaching the World Cup Finals and led 2–1 with nine minutes to go thanks to a brace from yours truly. But we had goalkeeping problems. Bill Brown was injured and Eddie Connachan had a bad night. We lost a late goal from a corner and went down in extra-time. Czechoslovakia went on to reach the Final itself.

Don't ask me why we didn't achieve more with the players we had at our disposal. They were the sort of players who would have blossomed on the stage of a major international competition. We were too wrapped up in beating England and fighting the rest of the world. There was a free-for-all with the Uruguayans at Hampden one night. I sat on the ball and watched it because I'd just returned from a suspension with Liverpool. The referee had to abandon a game against Austria the following year because of fighting. We were leading 4–1 at the time, but the scoreline didn't matter when there were scores to settle.

Our touring record said a lot for our approach to international football. I have told you before about Dave Mackay walking along a Turkish banquet table for a bet, and Jim Baxter collecting £1500 in wagers and blowing it all at an Irish racetrack. We didn't do things in half-measures on tour.

I can recall Mackay and Law reducing our so-called manager Andy Beattie to tears on a trip to Austria. When you visited a foreign country in those days, you did a bit of sight-seeing as well as a bit of playing and fighting.

You didn't particularly want to, but the local beauty spot was part of the itinerary. On this particular trip the Austrians were insistent that we see their best ski-run. It involved a coach journey halfway up a mountainside, followed by a walk to the top. Ideal preparation for an important football match!

As we set off up the mountain, Andy noticed that we were two short. Law and Mackay had decided that the bus station was far enough and had stayed put to talk to the locals. Andy sent his coach Dawson Walker down to fetch them, and they followed us up whistling an army marching song. Next day, they didn't even leave their rooms in case there was another day-trip. Andy couldn't drop them because he didn't pick the team. I'll never forget him standing in the hotel foyer in tears because he had no control over the players. It said a lot about the way our national team was run at that time.

17

Jimmy Johnstone – precocious talent who lived dangerously

Everywhere you looked on the team-bus there was a precocious talent, but everywhere you looked there was a larger-than-life character. Once after a defeat in Wales, Jimmy Johnstone sat on the bus aiming V-signs at passing Rangers fans. Some of them managed to get the back door open for a moment and it looked like we were in for a lynching before we got the driver to pull away. We lived dangerously.

I often wonder what I would do if I was in charge of a Scottish squad heading for the World Cup Finals. I can understand those managers who have whisked the players away from the hullabaloo in Scotland to the peace and quiet of a training camp. But I'm now of the opinion that that may be the worst possible thing to do. I think the best idea is to leave home as late as possible. In my experience a Scottish squad in isolation is a dangerous creature. The feeling within it boils up like water inside a kettle, and if it is left there too long, a kettle can explode.

2 A FUNNY OLD TEAM!

*In this chapter, Jimmy picks his best-ever team – with
laughs counting as much as football ability. Greavsie
remembers the men who not only could play a bit, but added
their own special humour to the funny old game.*

Some teams you pick for kicks, other teams you select for skill but here is a team that I have picked just for laughs. With every selection I have reached down into the cellar of my mind for a vintage memory that has made me chuckle . . . and with each memory there is a funny old goal involved.

In goal I have the one and only Pat Jennings. Every time I think of the big feller – he had hands as large as shovels – I giggle at the memory of a goal that he scored in the 1967 Charity Shield match against Manchester United at Old Trafford. Pat was the second most surprised man in the ground when his drop-kick from the Tottenham penalty area went first bounce into the back of the United net. Even more surprised was United goalkeeper Alex Stepney, who had been an interested spectator on the edge of the United penalty area when the ball suddenly sailed over his head.

In that deep Irish brogue of his, Pat described the goal like this: 'It was a once-in-a-lifetime thing. I'll never manage it again. The only reason I was able to get it into the net was because I had a really strong wind at my back. The funniest thing from my point of view was seeing Greavsie and Alan Gilzean – our two front runners – looking at each other in utter bewilderment wondering who to congratulate for the goal. They had their backs to me when I kicked the ball and had no idea

how it had got into the net. Then they looked back to see me dancing around like a boxer who had just delivered a knockout punch. I don't think they could believe their eyes.'

I remember saying to Alan Gilzean in what was our first match of the season, 'D'you realise, Gilly, that this makes Pat our top scorer!' We told the press after the match that this was a new tactic, and that Pat had been ordered to shoot every time he had the ball in his hands.

At right-back in my funny old team I have selected Peter Sillett, brother of Coventry boss John. Both were in the Chelsea squad when I first started out on my playing career. It was Peter, my old drinking pal, who scored the craziest goal I ever saw. It was against Everton at Stamford Bridge in the late fifties, and it gave me one of the best laughs I ever had on a football pitch – even though the goal was *against* us.

I still rate it one of the all-time unforgettable goals. If there had been action-replay machines around in those days I am sure it would still be shown as a comedy classic. A long shot from an Everton player slipped under the body of our England international goalkeeper Reg 'Give us a fag' Matthews, who used to smoke like a chimney.

Anyway, Reg scrambled up and chased after the ball, hotly challenged by our big, bold captain, Peter 'Give us a pint' Sillett, who thought he had a better chance of clearing it. They pounded neck and neck towards our goal. Reg won the race and then, instead of diving on the ball, elected to kick it away. He pivoted beautifully and cracked the ball dead centre – straight into the pit of Peter Sillett's stomach. The ball rebounded into the back of the net and Peter collapsed, holding his stomach. The rest of the Chelsea team – yours truly included – collapsed holding our stomachs as we laughed uncontrollably.

I select another golden oldie at left-back: Dennis Evans, who was an Arsenal favourite of the fifties. He scored one of the nuttiest goals of all time against Blackpool at Highbury in 1955. A 'phantom whistler' on the terraces blew what Dennis took to be the final whistle in the closing moments of the match. The Arsenal goalkeeper, Jack Kelsey, also thought it was the ref who whistled, and he was in the back of the net collecting his cap and gloves as Dennis casually stroked the

Below: Peter Sillett with his brother John, Chelsea full-backs in the late fifties

Right: Dennis Evans, left-back in Greavsie's funny old team

ball into the Arsenal net. The ref gave Blackpool a goal but, thank Evans, the game was already safe for Arsenal, who won 4–1. Just suppose it had been 0–0 when Dennis netted the ball. I reckon he would have got netted, too!

Wearing the number four shirt is my old Spurs and England colleague Alan Mullery. He reluctantly holds the record for the quickest own goal in League football history. Fulham's game against Sheffield Wednesday in 1961 was just thirty seconds old when he pushed a pass back from 20 yards to give goalkeeper Tony Macedo an early feel of the ball.

Left: Alan Mullery in his Fulham days – practising pass backs!

Below: Jack Charlton leaps to head the ball watched by Bobby Robson (*right*)

Tony was not expecting it, and was wrong-footed as the ball rolled past him into the net. Fulham started badly, and they got worse, finally losing 6–1.

Who else at centre-half but Jack 'The Giraffe' Charlton? The goal involving Jack was not scored by him, but it was his description of it that had me rolling around in the dressing room before one of our England training sessions. Leeds had played Liverpool at Anfield the previous weekend, and this was how Jack recalled one of the funniest goals ever witnessed on that famous ground: 'The game was into the second half, and we were a goal down in what was a vital championship match. There was snow on the ground, it was freezing cold and we were battling like crazy to try to get back into the game. A low ball went harmlessly through to Gary Sprake,

Bobby Moore . . . 'the finest defender I ever played with or against'

and as he bent to pick it up we all moved away down the field to start a counter-attack.

'As I ushered our back line forward there was an almighty roar from the Kop end behind our goal. I turned back to see Sprake standing on the edge of the eighteen-yard box with his hands covering his face. I looked in panic for the ball and there it was lying in the back of our net. All we Leeds players stood staring open-mouthed, wondering how the ball had got into the net when only seconds before it had been safely in Sprake's hands. I was near referee Jim Finney and politely inquired what had happened. Well, not *that* politely. In fact, I said something like, "What the blankety-blank's happened, ref?"

'Jim, one of the most respected of all referees, said in a matter-of-fact way: "Your goalkeeper has just thrown the ball into his own net." Then it was my turn to cover my face with my hands. But I managed to see the funny side of it when the Kop choir, quick as a flash, started to sing Des O'Connor's hit song, "Careless Hands".'

The number six shirt goes to the king of central defenders, Bobby Moore. The odd goal I associate with Bobby was scored *against* him while he was wearing the goalkeeper's jersey! It was during a League Cup semi-final second replay against Stoke City at Old Trafford in 1972. This is how Mooro, a good mate of mine as well as being the finest defender I ever played with or against, described it: 'I was in goal while our keeper Bobby Ferguson was off the pitch receiving treatment after being kicked in the head. Our right-back John McDowell underhit a back pass to me and the ball stuck in the mud. As I dashed forward to try to grab it at the feet of a Stoke forward, John made a desperate tackle and the referee awarded a penalty. Mickey Bernard took the penalty for Stoke. It was the only time in my life that I ever stood on the goal-line facing a penalty, and I felt like a man in front of a firing squad.

'I took a guess and dived to my right. I don't know who was more surprised – Mickey or me – when I managed to push the ball away, but before any of my team-mates could get to it Bernard had followed up and banged it into the net. The good news was that I had saved the penalty, but the bad news was that Stoke still managed to score and they went through to the Final.'

Kenny Dalglish comes in at number seven with a rare grin all over his face. He laughs at the memory of a goal he scored for Scotland against England at Hampden Park in 1976. The score was deadlocked at 1–1 when Kenny half-hit a shot from a tight angle on the right. Goalkeeper Ray Clemence went down on his knees to gather the ball, miscalculated its

Kenny Dalglish . . . a typical study of concentration

25

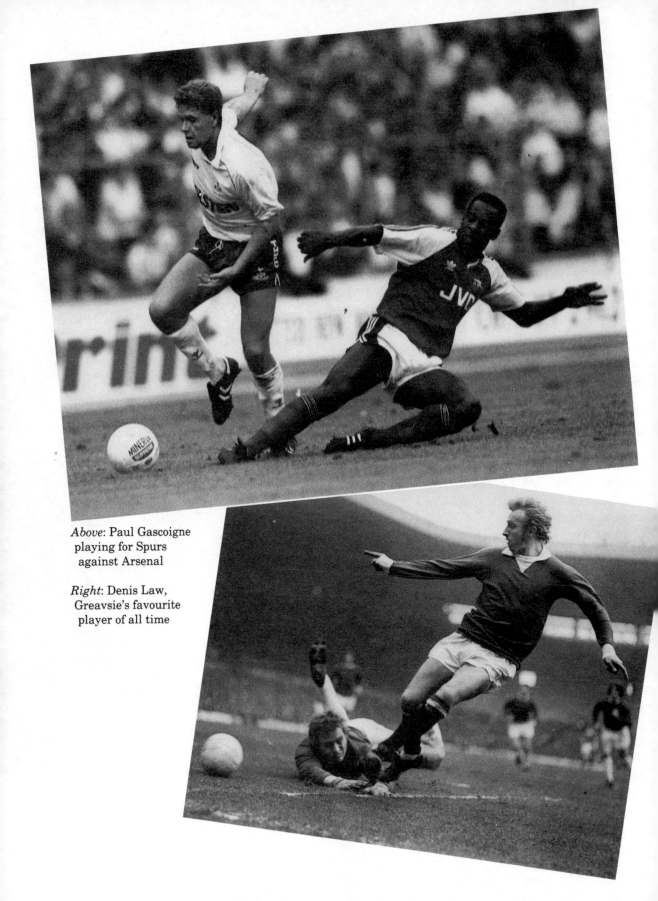

Above: Paul Gascoigne
playing for Spurs
against Arsenal

Right: Denis Law,
Greavsie's favourite
player of all time

pace and allowed it to roll between his legs and into the net. 'It was not a classic goal,' said canny Kenny. 'But they all count.' It was a precious goal for Scotland and gave them their first outright win in the Home Championships since 1967. There was not a single Scot at Hampden that day who did not consider it the funniest goal they had ever seen!

Paul Gascoigne, one of the few great characters in the modern game, gets the number eight shirt in my funny old team because of the goal he scored for Spurs in his home debut against Arsenal in 1988. He lost his boot in a tackle, but kept on going to sweep the loose ball into the net with his stockinged foot. He had really socked it to Arsenal! But the Gunners won the match 3–2.

Denis Law, my favourite player of all time, wears the number nine shirt. The laugh was on Denis when he scored seven goals for Manchester City yet finished on the losing side! He netted six goals against Luton in a third round FA Cup tie at Kenilworth Road in 1961, but the game was abandoned after 70 minutes because a monsoon had turned the pitch into a quagmire.

As the two teams waded back to the dressing rooms the referee apologised to Denis for having had to call off his one-man spectacular. The Lawman shrugged and said with typical humour: Don't worry about it, ref. I'm used to it now. The same thing happened to me when I was playing in a boys' match in Scotland after I'd scored six goals. I must be careful not to do it again!'

The match was replayed at Luton the following Wednesday – and Manchester City were beaten 3–1. Inevitably, Law scored City's goal. So his final tally was seven goals and defeat!

Terry Venables takes the number ten shirt thanks to a goal he collected while playing for Chelsea against AS Roma in a 1965 Fairs Cup tie at Stamford Bridge.

Chelsea had been awarded a free-kick just outside the penalty area, and Venner placed the ball as if he was going to take the kick. Then he made a great fuss of pacing out the stipulated ten yards, holding up his fingers in mime of a count as he approached the Roma 'wall' of defenders. The Italians, duped into thinking that Venner was going to have to return to the ball, opened the wall and allowed Venables through as he continued to count.

Suddenly Venner shouted to team-mate John Hollins, 'Give it now, John.' Hollins steered the ball through the hole in the middle of the wall and Venner coolly fired a low shot into the net for one of three goals he collected that night.

'Cheekie chappie' Terry Venables shares a joke with QPR club-mate, Terry Mancini

27

Ian Storey-Moore, number eleven in Greavsie's 'funny old team'

The number eleven shirt goes to Ian Storey-Moore, who was an exceptionally talented left-winger with Nottingham Forest and Manchester United before injury brought a premature end to his career. Ian's novel goal that wins him a place in my funny old team came in the last minute of a sixth round FA Cup tie against Everton in 1967.

The scores were level and the match into injury-time when Forest partners John Winfield and Frank Wignall combined to thread the ball through to Ian, who was fifteen yards out from the Everton goal. He took a snap shot and the ball hit defender John Hurst. He collected the rebound and fired in a second shot that was pushed out by goalkeeper Andy Rankin. Moore nodded the clearance against the bar and then dashed forward to head the rebound into the net for a remarkable winning goal.

The substitute's shirt goes to Alan Hudson for a goal that wasn't but was! Hudson spirited a 'ghost goal' for Chelsea against Ipswich at Stamford Bridge in 1970. He hammered a shot into the side netting and was astonished to see referee Roy Capey pointing to the centre circle to signal a goal that put Chelsea on the way to a 2–1 victory. 'I didn't argue with the ref,' said Hudson. 'You've got to be a bit stupid to protest if you're being awarded a goal.'

On the very same day as Hudson's ghost goal there was an astonishing incident at Filbert Street where Leicester City were at home in a League match against Portsmouth. Pompey striker Jim Storrie headed the ball wide of goalkeeper Peter Shilton. The ball hit the stanchion at the back of the net and bounced back into play. The referee waved play on, thinking the ball had hit a post. 'I couldn't believe it,' said Shilton after Leicester had won the match 2–0. 'The ball definitely went into the net. But my team-mates would have shot me if I'd chased after the ref and told him he should have given Portsmouth a goal.'

My substitute goalkeeper has to be my old England team-mate Gordon Banks. Every time we see each other he reminds me of a goal I scored against him for Spurs during a League match against Leicester City. I'll let Gordon tell the story: 'It was the craziest goal ever allowed. Spurs were awarded a penalty and Greavsie elected himself to take it. There was hardly any grass around and I had gone back inside the goal to wipe all the muck off my hands ready to face the penalty. Jimmy, the cheeky so-and-so, sidefooted the ball into the other corner of the net while I was bending down.

'I don't know who was more surprised when

Brian Clough . . . 'one of the most prolific goal-snatchers in football history'

the referee signalled a goal, Jimmy or me. What made it worse was instead of telling the ref he was wrong even my own team-mates were falling about laughing.'

The manager of my give-us-a-laugh team is none other than 'The Guv'nor' Brian Clough.

He was one of the most prolific goal-snatchers in football history before a knee injury forced his retirement at the age of 28. There has rarely been a more self-confident character than Cloughie, on or off the pitch. Early in his career at Middlesbrough a young winger complained to the manager that Cloughie – his team-mate – had knocked him off the ball in front of an open goal and scored himself. When asked about the incident Brian shrugged and said in his matter-of-fact way, 'Well, I'm better at it than he is.' End of conversation.

Cloughie and I played alongside each other when he made his two appearances for England back in 1959. I remember one hilarious incident during the second game against Sweden. There was a goalmouth scramble with Cloughie trying desperately to force the ball over the Swedish goal-line. A defender tripped him up and Cloughie found himself sitting on the ball and unable to get off. He said later, 'I felt as if I was hatching the ruddy thing!'

We lost the match 3–2 and Cloughie carried the can. He was never selected again. That was no laughing matter.

Greavsie's 'funny old team'

1: Pat Jennings
2: Peter Sillett
3: Dennis Evans
4: Alan Mullery
5: Jack Charlton
6: Bobby Moore
7: Kenny Dalglish
8: Paul Gascoigne
9: Denis Law
10: Terry Venables
11: Ian Storey-Moore
12: Alan Hudson
14: Gordon Banks
Manager: Brian Clough

So that's my team just for laughs – and a very select side it is, too! But I cannot let this chapter on funny old goals go without sharing some more memories with you of goals that had me giggling. Top of the list has to be a

goal I scored that had the Saint tearing at the wig he wears!

Come with me back to the sixties and a First Division match between Tottenham and Liverpool at White Hart Lane. We were awarded a free-kick at the inside left position just outside the penalty box. Terry Venables and I stood over the ball and pretended to argue as to which of us should take it. While Terry was still arguing and gesticulating, I suddenly curled a shot into the far corner of the net, with goalkeeper Tommy Lawrence rooted on his line trying to organise the wall in front of him.

The Saint led a posse of players in a protest march on the referee, but he insisted that the goal had to stand. Venner and I could hardly move for laughing at the way Liverpool had fallen for our con trick.

Liverpool's legendary manager Bill Shankly saw me coming out of our dressing room after the match. Shanks was down the far end of the corridor and shouted in that rasping bagpipes of a voice of his, 'Jimmy Greaves – you're a wee rascal . . . a pickpocket. There was only one thing wrong with you today, son – you were wearing the wrong colour shirt. It should have been red.'

Then he added with a chuckle, 'You won't thieve anything from us at Anfield. We'll put the handcuffs on you.' Sure enough, I hardly got a kick when we next played at Liverpool. In fact (along with a lot of other footballers) I was never once on a winning side at Anfield throughout my career. Shanks would not stand for it!

Another goal that always makes me smile when I think about it was the one described to me by Howard Kendall during his days as a player with Everton. He told me: 'We had two Newtons in our squad at Everton, Henry and Keith. In their tactical talk before the match the West Brom players were told to attack Henry Newton on his left side. "He's got no left foot; so when he's in possession force him to his left all the time," the coach stressed.

'West Brom's Graham Lovett was the first to get tested by an aggressive run from Newton and he duly jockeyed him out to the left, making sure he was unable to switch the ball to his right foot. Then suddenly Newton let fly with a rocketing left-foot shot from thirty yards that was a goal from the moment he connected.

'I was in hearing distance of Lovett as he looked to the touchline bench with his arms opened wide to express his astonishment. "Thought you said he only had a right foot," he shouted. Back came the reply, "It's the wrong bloody Newton!" The goalscorer was *Keith* Newton. Henry wasn't even playing!'

A goal story that always brings tears to my eyes is the one that Tommy 'The Charmer' Harmer tells. Tommy was a Tom Thumb of a player who paraded his bewildering ball skills with Tottenham before winding down his career with Chelsea.

Tom, a midfield schemer who scored only a handful of goals throughout his distinguished career, was playing in a vital end-of-season promotion match for Chelsea at Sunderland.

This is how Harmer recalled scoring the goal that earned Tommy Docherty's Chelsea promotion back to the First Division: 'There was an inswinging corner and the ball hit me and went into the net off what I can only describe as my private parts. It hurt like hell but it was worth it, even though I had to put up with being called "the cock of the north" and "the man with the secret weapon".'

Tommy had the greatest game of his life when Bill Nicholson had his first match as manager of Tottenham at White Hart Lane in October, 1958. Spurs gave Bill Nick an incredible welcome with a 10–4 victory over

'It's Newton!' But which one? This is Keith Newton in his Everton days

31

Everton, and Harmer had a hand – or rather a well-directed foot – in nine of the goals, including one he scored himself with a thunderbolt shot from outside the penalty area. It was the only time in his career that he scored from more than 15 yards.

As he came off at the end, the tiny tot – he was only 5 feet 4 inches tall – gave Bill Nicholson a wry smile and said, 'Don't expect that sort of result every week, boss!'

For my last story in this goal gourmet's feast I am crossing the Atlantic to South America and what is alleged to be a true account of an extraordinary incident involving Brazil's wonder winger Roberto Rivelino. He is credited with the fastest goal of all time. The ball was passed to him from the kick-off in a Brazilian League match and he hammered in a shot from the centre circle. The goalkeeper was on his knees praying for a successful game at the time, and the ball whizzed over his head and into the net. The goal was timed at three seconds.

It was reported that a spectator then came running on to the pitch with a pistol in his hand and fired six shots into the ball. I understand the goalkeeper was later given the bullet!

I know this all sounds far-fetched, but nutty things do happen in South American football. It was in Uruguay in 1957 that a goal was credited to a mongrel dog. The ball was running loose in the penalty area when the dog came racing on to the pitch and 'nosed' it into the net. Next day an advertisement was placed in the local newspaper by a fan with a sense of humour. It asked the owner of the dog to sell the goal-poaching pooch to the home team!

Finally, just how important can a name be when it comes to football? Not a lot you would imagine ... but it could prove more than a little embarrassing if your last name happened to be something like **Bum** and you earned your livelihood through playing professional football! Those delightfully sympathetic chaps on the terraces and in the stands would simply split their sides laughing at you ... that's for sure! Without doubt, they'd hurl constant torrents of abuse in your particular direction and show little or no mercy, while deriving great pleasure from ridiculing you at every available opportunity, wouldn't they?

BUM KICKS TWO GOALS IN SOUTH KOREAN VICTORY

No, the above headline is not a misprint nor a figment of the editor of this book's fertile imagination. It did, in all honesty, appear within the sports pages of Thailand's *Bangkok Post!* Koo Sang Bum is, in fact, a South Korean international whose two goals in a 2–0 victory for Lucky Goldstar FC over Indonesia hit the headlines in January, 1989.

From all accounts Bum is a bouncy, attack-minded winger who, although he's a great advocate of that tackle from behind which is so unpopular in Britain, would definitely get a real kick out of displaying his skills in the English First Division. With which club would Bum be best placed and most likely to demonstrate his distinctive style of play? Having cast my naked eye over the league table from top to bottom, I quickly came to the conclusion that, with a name like Koo Sang Bum, he would feel definitely at home and be a big hit with the fans at where else but – Arse-nal!

3 TROUBLESOME TYKES!

Yorkshiremen get the reputation of being dour and lacking in humour. But that's not the Saint's memories of some of the great characters and laugh-a-minute trips around the grounds of England, in his association with Yorkshire clubs.

From the days in the sixties when Big Jack and Norman used to kick me from end-to-end of Elland Road, to the days in the seventies when I joined Jack at Sheffield Wednesday, the great White Rose county of Yorkshire has played its full part in my football education.

People get the wrong idea of Yorkshire folk. They think they live their lives like Geoffrey Boycott batted. I'm sure the late Don Revie's great side would have been heralded as great entertainers if they'd played in London, instead of Leeds. They weren't the dour bunch that the rest of the country said they were.

I met Don on a golfing holiday in Spain a couple of years ago and he and his wife invited us to have dinner with them. We talked about those great days when Leeds and Liverpool fought for supremacy in the English game, and he and Bill Shankly were such rivals.

I never knew before but Shanks would often phone Don up at about eight o'clock on a Sunday morning when he and Elsie were still dozing. 'Another good result for you yesterday, I see Don,' Shanks would shout down the phone; and a bleary-eyed Revie would reach for the bedside lamp mumbling, 'Yes, and you too, Bill.' Shanks would then rant on for half an hour about how magnificent Liverpool had been, with Don unable to get a word in edgeways. Then before he had a chance to say anything about Leeds' display, Shanks was saying his goodbyes and the Revies were returning thankfully to their lie-in.

Don would do anything for Leeds . . . and was often accused of going over the top to pressurise the opposition. Certainly his team knew how to moan. They appealed against every decision given to the opposition and I'm sure it was their moaning which took the gloss from what was an outstanding Revie regime.

Don was like a father figure to all the Leeds lads and at his funeral in Scotland, there were tears in the eyes of such as Jack Charlton, Billy Bremner and Norman Hunter – men who appreciated what the big fella did for United.

Don's bingo sessions on the eve of a big match were legendary. It always amazed me how he could control the exuberance of professional footballers such as he had under him. Other clubs used to laugh at Leeds pre-match entertainment – but it was usually the Don and his men who had the last laugh on the pitch.

They knew how to argue though did Leeds. They could play all right – but that wasn't all they could do. The Football League sent a circular round to managers about dissent following complaints that Leeds and other teams were intimidating officials. Shanks called us in for a special meeting and said, 'If a decision goes against you, just walk away, boys. I don't want any talking back to the referees.' We fol-

Bill Shankly proudly holds the Charity Shield after Liverpool beat Leeds United in 1974

lowed his orders for two or three games, but didn't win any of them. Leeds were going clear at the top, so Shanks called another meeting. 'Remember what I said about walking away from referees, boys? Well, next time an official gives a bad decision, mob him!!!' Our results picked up straight away.

Anything we did in response to Leeds United was only a mark of respect for the way they were developing. They drew 0–0 at our place one night to clinch the Championship. We wouldn't have scored in a week. They went on to succeed us as the number one team in the country, and to play football the likes of which I'd never seen. Our greatest day against them was my big day at Wembley in the 1965 FA Cup Final. Don and Shanks were sat almost side by side on the manager's bench. If only you could have sat between them, eh? There's a story that Leeds United's coloured winger Albert Johanneson was closing down Chrissie Lawler as he tried to play the ball down the line, and Don's trainer Les Cocker shouted out, 'Go on Albert, you've got him snookered.' Quick as a flash, Bill shouted back: 'Snookered behind the black, eh Don?'

I'll never forget our boss ranting on before the game about the Leeds dressing room being locked. We had open house that day. Jimmy Tarbuck and Frankie Vaughan wandered in to keep us all relaxed and amused. There was even a television crew filming us. Shanks was saying that they were locked away, scared stiff with all their superstitions. They were a very superstitious lot. The ten minutes before you kicked off against Leeds was a real carry-on. Everybody was doing something. I always remember the last thing was Billy Bremner running over to the dug-out and giving his wedding ring to Les Cocker. You knew they were ready to start then.

Maybe that last half-hour before the Wembley Final epitomised the different charac-

Billy Bremner – always ran over to the dug-out to give his wedding ring to Les Cocker just before the kick-off

ters of Leeds and Liverpool in those days. Our dressing-room door was open to all and sundry – they had a protective shield around them. Sitting in that Spanish restaurant with Don, he admitted to me that his only mistake was not letting his players off the leash earlier than he did. He said he'd been too cautious and careful. When he gave them a free rein they were tremendous, as good as any modern club team. All of us outside of Yorkshire sometimes forget just how good they were.

I crossed the Pennines again in 1978, this time to team up with Jack Charlton, who had taken over as manager of Sheffield Wednesday. I was clearing up my problems with Portsmouth, and had been working on a television programme for Granada in Manchester when Jack offered me a chance to return to football as a coach.

He employed a good pal of mine, Maurice Setters, too. His trainer was another great character, Tony Toms, who had survived the departure of Lennie Ashurst. Together we spent one of my happiest years in football at Hillsborough before my television career started to take off.

I'd met Tony a year earlier when Lennie had invited me to join them on a pre-season trip to an army camp in Devon. It turned out that Tomsy was a former Marine instructor who was in his element on an assault course. He was the man that Stallone based 'Rambo' upon. Built like a Bondi lifeguard, he had fought in Suez and Malaya, and was no great lover of footballers. He was the club physiotherapist, but refused to administer treatment to any player who still had all his limbs dangling from the correct places on his body. He nearly had a fit when Rodger Wylde started to use a hairdrier in the dressing room.

The fact was that football was the only sport he didn't know the first thing about. As an army PT expert, he was an ace at just about everything. He could beat me at badminton playing left-handed, and often started training sessions with a game of touch-rugby to show what he could do with a ball in his hands. But he couldn't play football to save his life.

He used to take fitness classes in the big Hillsborough gymnasium in his spare time. He had sessions for men and sessions for women. Sometimes he'd offer Maurice or I a fiver to take the men, then turn up for the women in a brand-new tracksuit dripping with after-shave. The club were picking up a cut of his takings, but he was always a little vague on the numbers attending the classes. One night the chairman turned up to see for himself. Next morning we asked Tomsy what had happened. 'There was no problem,' he said. 'I just kept them moving so he couldn't count them.'

Tony loved coming the sergeant major to the players. When one or two of them complained that the assault-course rope slide was a bit dangerous, he shouted back, 'Yes, that's what my grandma said before she did it.' He caught Tommy Tynan slacking during a weights session on one occasion, and threw him through some swing-doors. I thought he was never going to come down, he hurled him so far.

When Tomsy and Len Ashurst first arrived at Sheffield Wednesday they were on the verge of slipping into the Fourth Division, and were in desperate need of a win to stop the slide. Tony assured Len he had the solution, and took the players out on to the Yorkshire Moors for a night. They spent the night sleeping under the stars in sleeping-bags – SAS character-building, they were told.

In the early hours of the morning, Tomsy overheard three or four of them plotting. They were discussing whether or not they could find their way to a road if they were to hit him over the head with a brick. After a while the voice of reason was raised by one of the senior players: 'We had better not – what if we didn't knock him out, he'd kill us!'

Anyway Wednesday won that match and escaped relegation with the threat of further visits to the Moors hanging over them. It seems to have been part of the Hillsborough battle-plan ever since, although I can't see big Ron Atkinson fancying it!

Tony Toms was a brilliant guy to work with and an expert in his field. He now trains the former sprinter Donna Hartley in her body-building career, and runs a successful gym in Sheffield. Maurice Setters and I once went to stay at his cottage in the hills. It had no central heating, and he just threw us down a couple of blankets and invited us to bed down on the floor. We were trying to get his dog to

lie at our feet, we were so cold. He heard us complaining eventually, and handed us a balaclava each. I think Tomsy was still fighting the War.

Anyone who can plant a smacker on Ted Croker's cheek in front of over 40,000 people at Wembley has to be a bit different – and Brian Clough is certainly that. Cloughie epitomises the old adage, 'Love him or hate him – but you can't ignore him.'

He's a Yorkshireman, you know. Born in that unlovely city of Middlesbrough when it was part of the White Rose county. I reckon Cloughie was a thorn! Whatever you say

It takes all sorts! Cloughie needed his special sense of humour when sacked by Leeds after 44 days

about the old boy he does have a very special sense of humour. Mind you, he needed it when Leeds sacked him after forty-four days.

It was during that infamous period of his life that he told Eddie Gray: 'If you'd been a racehorse, I'd have had you put down years ago!' That might sound callous, and it certainly didn't go down too well with Leeds fans to whom the brilliant Gray was a folk hero, but it was his way of saying that the Scottish winger was doing well to be playing at all after an appalling run of injuries.

Northern folk can be blunt to say the least – they're almost proud to list it among their credentials – and Clough is a past master of the cutting comment. Before one game in Rumania he lined all his players up against a wall at a press conference because he said they 'deserved to be shot at'!

For the next ten minutes he proceeded to pull his players to bits in front of everyone – even suggesting to Kenny Burns it was good of him to turn up as he thought he'd be out 'nicking meters'!

As the players squirmed in shock-horror and wondered what was coming next, Cloughie rounded on the mortified Larry Lloyd with a question. 'Hey Larry, I want you to tell me something.'

'What's that, boss?'

'I want you to tell me who won two caps for England on the same day.'

'I've no idea, boss. That's impossible, isn't it?'

'No you did: your first and your . . . last!'

Few managers are lost for words, especially these days when they're constantly in demand for radio and television interviews. Obviously some are more adept at it than others and I often wonder how the old Bradford City manager Ivor Powell would have coped with the barrage of questions. Ivor suffered from a surfeit of spoonerisms – you know what that is, when the words don't quite come out as they're supposed to do. A bit like Greavsie when he's trying to extol the virtues of Scottish goalies!

After one good sequence of results by Bradford, Ivor was asked by a local journalist to explain the upsurge in form and back came the reply: 'It's all down to the harmonium in the dressing room.' I wonder who was playing it!

At the end of the season he was presented with some silverware by the supporters' club and he thanked them for their gift of a silver salvo! I bet that went off with a bang!

One of Bradford's greatest characters in recent years has been Bobby Campbell. Now big Bobby will admit to you that he was certainly no choirboy in his youth, in fact his career was saved from disaster when he joined Bradford after some unhappy episodes at Aston Villa, Halifax, Huddersfield, Sheffield United and even Brisbane City in Australia.

To Bobby's credit he buckled down at Bradford and went on to become their record goalscorer in League football with 121 goals in his two spells at Valley Parade. But good or bad Bobby was always a character and you'll hear plenty of stories about him if you go to Yorkshire.

During his time at Huddersfield one of his bosses was Tom Johnston, that canny old fox who was one of the most astute and knowledgeable men in the game. Tom was getting on a bit, so you can imagine when the weather turned nasty he wasn't all that keen to get out on the training ground with the lads.

One particular nasty morning Tom decided he needed to be by his phone just in case it rang, so he told Bobby to take the session. 'You saw what I did yesterday, just do exactly the same,' he told him.

Fatal words. Bobby ran the whole team up a hillside adjacent to the ground and back down until they were all caked in mud. Then he took them into the car park, opened the door to Tom Johnston's shining motor, clambering through one side and out the other, followed by every single player!

'Well I saw you get in and out of your car and you told me to follow you exactly,' grinned Bobby to his spluttering boss.

People say there isn't as much humour in football these days – and that's probably right, although I'm sure there are a few quips whenever Paul Gascoigne plays in a game with Neil Midgley as ref.

Who'd be a referee? And who'd be a linesman? Now they are jobs for masochists.

It was good to hear a story about a linesman with a definite sense of humour recently. The only black official on the Football League list is Trevor Moore who comes from Bradford – well he would, wouldn't he? Trevor was running the line in a pre-season game at Scarborough and the referee was getting a bit of hassle from 'Boro's manager Neil Warnock who kept jumping in and out of his dug-out to protest at decisions. Twice the referee warned Warnock that any more dissent and he could send him off.

The next time he leapt to his feet Trevor was there first. 'Get back there. Now you've had it in black AND white!' he said. All parties saw the funny side of it and the situation was defused.

John Charles, the Welsh giant

A smile has been put back on the face of the game by author Fred Eyre, who bases his stories on his own failures as a footballer. As an undistinguished full-back who must have played for more clubs than George Best has been in, Fred never won the right to glowing reports from the press.

On 7 March, 1970, he played his one and only league game for Bradford Park Avenue. They lost 5–0 at Swansea. Reporter Stanley Pearson of the *Bradford Telegraph and Argus* wrote: 'Little was seen of new boy Eyre in the first half – and even less in the second half!'

The following week he posed the question: 'Will Bradford be at full strength on Saturday – or will Eyre play?'

That must have done wonders for Fred's ego! Anyway he didn't play and at the end of that season Bradford were kicked out of the Football League, as were his next club, Southport.

Fred certainly wasn't a good luck charm.

Someone who never played for Bradford Park Avenue or Southport – or come to think of it, Accrington or Gateshead – was John Charles. That's because King John was one of the greats: a legend in Italy for his feats with Juventus, and in Britain for his deeds in the colours of Leeds United and Wales.

It was always a matter of much argument as to whether the 'Gentle Giant' was better as a centre-half or centre-forward. He was magnificent in both positions, of course. The first time he moved up front he had a bit of a stinker and the team was well and truly trounced.

'I thought that was it and that I'd never play there again, but to my astonishment the manager, Major Frank Buckley, kept me there for the next game and I got a hat-trick. I was walking past the Queens Hotel in the centre of Leeds the next day when a voice shouted to me. It was our chairman, Mr Sam Bolton. He said I'd done so well and they were so pleased with me that I had qualified for a bonus.

'As a youngster I suppose my eyes lit up at the prospect until he told me to go and help myself to three gallons of petrol that were stored away in a garage for me! "But I haven't got a car, Mr Bolton," I explained.

' "Well never mind you can always save up for one," he said and walked away.'

Talking of great philosophers, Lincoln City once had a manager called Bill Anderson. One particularly windy Saturday afternoon he advised his players to 'keep the high balls low'.

He also impeached them to make any 50-50 balls 60-40 in their favour, adding: 'If you're going to veer, veer straight.' Now that takes some doing.

Another from the old school of management was Angus Seed who had charge of Barnsley in the early fifties. He subscribed to a theory that it would be better for his players to train all week without a ball. The idea being they would all be hungry for it on the Saturday. As Danny Blanchflower observed later: 'It sounded fine in practice. The trouble was when we did get the ball we didn't know what the hell to do with it.'

Tim Ward, who succeeded Seed, had a sense of humour though. He called over a player after one match and told him: 'I thought you had two good runs tonight.'

'Thanks boss.'

'Yes, one up the tunnel and one down it.'

The first time Barnsley played under floodlights was at Falkirk, a match which was part of the deal that took Barnsley's popular winger Johnny Kelly to Scotland.

Before the game Ward asked his captain, Norman Smith, if he had ever played under such conditions before. 'Yes,' came the reply, 'at Arsenal. And if I win the toss tomorrow night I'll play with the moon at our backs.'

They're naturally funny folk at Barnsley. When Skinner Normanton, that legendary hard man, clattered one little winger into the ground for the umpteenth time, one wag shouted to the trainer: 'Don't pick him up. Bury the bugger.'

It's even been known for a St John's Ambulanceman at Oakwell to ask a player for his autograph as he's carrying him off on a stretcher with a broken leg!

On another occasion, when play seemed to be concentrated around the same area of the pitch for a long time, one spectator roared his disapproval: 'Will you stop playing behind that bloody pillar!'

4 JEEPERS KEEPERS!

They say you have to be daft to be a goalkeeper – and Greavsie adds fuel to the argument as he picks his Top Ten goalies, adding of course some of the hilarious behind-the-scenes stories of the men who have worn the yellow jersey with distinction.

The remarkable thing about Peter Shilton's record run as England goalkeeper is that he should, by rights, have at least another twenty caps to his name.

He became the puppet of an indecisive selection policy when Ron Greenwood was England manager. Shilts had to play a game of musical chairs for the goalkeeping job with his great rival Ray Clemence. Peter got so frustrated at one point that he even asked not to be considered for international duty.

I had always found Greenwood a deeply intelligent but strangely indecisive manager when I played under him at West Ham. He took this wavering mood into his role as England boss. Greenwood was unable to make up his mind whether Shilton or Clemence was the better man, and so he introduced the silly system of playing them in alternative matches.

Clemence was a first-rate goalkeeper, but I never had any doubts that Shilton had the edge over him during what were the peak years of his career with Nottingham Forest.

Instead of overtaking Bobby Moore's record of 108 England caps, Peter should now have been poised to beat the world record cap collection set by green-fingered Pat Jennings.

Pat played his 119th and final match for Northern Ireland against Brazil in the World Cup Finals on 12 June, 1986, on which memorable day he also celebrated his 41st birthday.

I am convinced that Shilts will go on to beat the Jennings' total of international appearances. He plays with a poise and a purpose that spreads confidence throughout the England defence, and he is worth a goal start to England just by his reassuring presence on the goal-line.

Goalkeepers are better preserved than outfield players, and Shilts will be 40 when the World Cup Finals kick off. There will not be a fitter forty-year-old in the land.

Peter was a fitness fanatic when I used to play against him centuries ago, and to this day he follows the same vigorous exercise routine. It has shaped a physique which earns him the dressing-room nickname of 'Tarzan'.

He started his career with his local club, Leicester City, as understudy to the great Gordon Banks. Gordon told me back in 1965 that there was a kid coming along at Leicester who could be a world-beater. He was talking about young Shilts.

Peter had to live in Gordon's shadow, but then followed him into the Leicester City goal and later succeeded him at Stoke City in 1974 after a car smash had cruelly ended the Banks reign as the king of goalkeepers.

Peter Shilton and some of his England caps

Shilton's career came to something of a standstill at Stoke, but it was given the kick of life when he moved to Nottingham Forest where Brian Clough and Peter Taylor gave him the motivation he needed.

Forest were a formidable side when Shilts took over in goal. With his arrival, they became almost unbeatable. When Cloughie bought him he also bought the League Championship and put down a deposit on the European Cup. He was that big an influence on the team.

It is a well-known fact in the game that Shilts has been one of the highest-paid players in the land for more than a dozen years, becoming a gold-fingered player with Southampton and then Derby County. But he has earned every penny with goalkeeping that has been of the highest possible standard.

I have always rated Gordon Banks and Pat Jennings as the greatest goalkeepers against whom I ever played. Sentiment is persuading me to say they are still a fingertip ahead of Shilts, but he may force me to make a reassessment before his remarkable career is over.

This is how I rate the Top Ten goalkeepers of my lifetime. I give two lists, one for the immediate post-war years and the other for modern goalkeepers:

1940s–1950s

1: Frank Swift (England)
2: Jack Kelsey (Wales)
3: Ted Ditchburn (England)
4: Bert Trautmann (Germany)
5: Bert Williams (England)
6: Tommy Younger (Scotland)
7: Harry Gregg (Northern Ireland)
8: Gil Merrick (England)
9: Sam Bartram (England)
10: Eddie Hopkinson (England)

Tommy Younger (Scotland)

1960s–1980s

1: Pat Jennings (Northern Ireland)
2: Gordon Banks (England)
3: Peter Shilton (England)
4: Neville Southall (Wales)
5: Ray Clemence (England)
6: Peter Bonetti (England)
7: Ron Springett (England)
8: Alex Stepney (England)
9: Phil Parkes (England)
10: Bob Wilson (Scotland)

Right: Neville Southall (Wales)

Below: Pat Jennings (Northern Ireland) and Ray Clemence (England) performing a country dance!

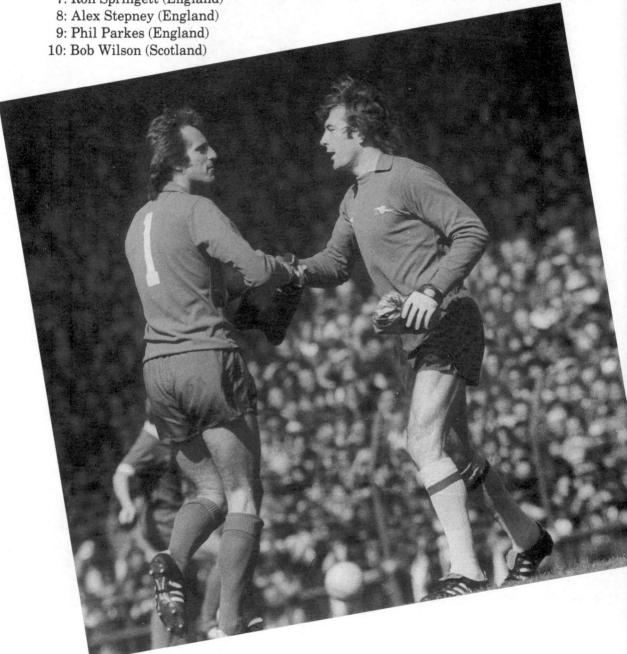

I had no hesitation in making the legendary Frank Swift my number one choice in the 1940s–1950s list, but I anguished over having to leave out goalkeepers of the calibre of Alan Hodgkinson, George Farm, Colin McDonald and Ray Wood.

The number one spot in the modern list gave me the biggest headache, Pat Jennings finally getting the nod over Gordon Banks because of his extraordinary consistency over a stretch of more than 1000 games. Gordon would, I am sure, have reached the same sort of appearances milestone but for the crash that ended his career.

Neville Southall has been one of the finest of all goalkeepers for the past five years and challenges the great Jack Kelsey for the rating of the number one goalkeeper produced by Wales.

I have been a tongue-in-cheek critic of Scottish goalkeepers for years, but there were a dozen outstanding Scottish goalkeepers challenging for a place in my Top Ten list. They included David Harvey, Jim Leighton and my old Spurs team-mate Bill Brown.

Ronnie Simpson, Celtic's last line of defence in the 1967 European Cup-winning team after FA Cup success with Newcastle United, narrowly missed out in both lists after a safe-handling career that spanned twenty years from the late forties.

Two Liverpool goalkeepers on my shortlist were Tommy 'The Flying Pig' Lawrence and Bruce Grobbelaar. Both have been idols of Anfield, but were just unable to make it into my Top Ten list.

I am sure you will have your own favourites for the goalkeeping hall of fame, and will doubtless disagree with some of my selections. But one thing's for sure – British football could not be in better hands.

I cannot let this study of goalkeepers go without passing on to you some of my all-time 'golden oldie' favourite tales from the dressing room. These are stories about goalkeepers that have been passed on down the decades from old pros to newcomers. . . .

Albert Iremonger was one of the most astonishing characters ever to pull on a goalkeeper's jersey. He played for Notts County for twenty-one years during the first quarter of the century, and he became such a legendary figure that they named a Nottingham street after him.

He used to think nothing of coming out of his penalty area to take free-kicks, throw-ins and even corner kicks. 'Long Albert' – he was 6 feet 5 inches tall and as lean as a lamppost – was an excitable man who used to have running arguments with referees. He once made such a nuisance of himself in a match at West Ham that a woman came on to the pitch and thumped him over the head with an umbrella. 'That'll teach you to get on with the game,' she told him.

Albert always had an answer, no matter what the situation. He looked up to the sky and said to the woman, 'Let's borrow your umbrella, love. It looks like it's going to rain.'

When a referee was going to send off one of his team-mates for a brutal tackle, Albert ran from his goal-line to the opposite penalty area to implore: 'For goodness sake, ref, don't send him off. There'll be nothing left in our pockets when we get to our dressing room.'

In the days of famous sprinter Harry Hutchins – the Linford Christie of his time – Albert followed a referee to the halfway line disputing a goal that had been awarded to Tottenham at White Hart Lane. The exasperated referee looked into the face of the towering inferno that was Albert and said, 'Iremonger, I'm warning you just once. I'm sending you off if you're not back on your goal-line in 10 seconds.'

'Who d'you think I am?' replied our Albert. 'Harry blinking Hutchins?'

Albert Iremonger . . . a legendary figure who had a Nottingham street named after him

His favourite form of protest was to sit on the ball and refuse to return it after any debatable decision against him. He once clasped his long arms round a rival forward after conceding a goal. 'Give over, Albert, and let me get on with t'game,' said the player.

'Oh, no,' said our Albert. 'I'm holding you hostage until t'game's over. I'm not having you knocking any more goals past me.'

I hope you have now got a mental picture of Albert because I am coming to one of my favourite football stories that is absolutely true. . . .

Our Albert elected himself penalty-taker in a match against Sheffield Wednesday at Hillsborough. He took a twenty-yard run up to the ball and hammered it with all his considerable might. His shot hit the crossbar with such force that it rebounded past all the players as far as the halfway line.

There was a Keystone Cops-style chase back, led by the long-striding Albert. A Sheffield Wednesday player managed to help the ball on its way into the Notts County penalty area, and then a breathless Albert arrived on the scene just ahead of a mad scramble of

players. He elected to kick the ball wide for a corner but instead managed to smash it into the back of his own net!

Bill 'Fatty' Foulke was around at about the same time as our Albert, and these two between them did more than anybody to popularise the old football saying that 'all goalkeepers are crazy.'

Foulke was a mountain of a man, 6 feet 3 inches tall and weighing nearly 23 stone at his peak. For all his size, he was as light as a ballerina on his feet, and was sufficiently mobile to win an England cap and two FA Cup winners' medals with Sheffield United.

He could fist the ball almost as far as he could kick it, and the story goes that a Sheffield United scout was watching him play for a Derbyshire colliery team when, attempting to punch the ball away, he missed and knocked out a rival forward's front teeth.

When the scout explained what had happened the Sheffield United manager is said to have replied: "E'll do for me.'

Big Bill was anything but a gentle giant. He had a volcanic temper, and once at Liverpool picked up a forward by his heels and hung him head-first above the ground, threatening to drop him, until he was persuaded by team-mates to let him down gently.

When he was invited to a Sheffield theatre during a United Cup run the management had to make three seats into one for him. They laid on a spread before the show, and Big Bill was the first to arrive. He had demolished food meant for six players before any of his team-mates arrived.

He once punched a hole in the dressing-room door in temper at a referee's decision, and threatened to do similar damage to Tom Kirkham, a referee from Burslem, after he had awarded a disputed goal against Sheffield United in the 1902 FA Cup Final at Crystal Palace.

Foulke came out of the United dressing room stark naked and chased Kirkham along the corridor. The referee had the good sense to lock himself in his room until the raging bull had been returned to base.

'I have never seen a sight quite like it,' said Mr Kirkham. The mind boggles.

Foulke wound down his career with Chelsea, by which time his weight had gone up past 25 stone. Time had not improved his temper. He once picked up an opponent and hurled him bodily into the back of the net.

The referee was the renowned J. T. Howcroft, of Bolton, who recalled: 'I was not fool enough or brave enough to send Bill off. I had been a linesman in the 1902 FA Cup Final and knew what he was like when he was riled.

'When I awarded a penalty he came looking for my scalp, but the Chelsea captain, H. T. Roberton, ordered him back to the goal-line. He didn't take his eyes off me the whole time the penalty was being taken. But you could not hold a grudge against him. He was such a cheerful, likeable fellow once his temper was under control.'

Sadly, I now have to introduce a sad note. Big Bill hit tough times at the end of his career, and had to suffer the humiliation of working as a sideshow attraction with a travelling fair.

'Penny a shot, three pence back if you score against the famous Fatty Foulke,' was the showmaster's cry. Poor old Bill caught pneumonia standing out in the rain at the fair, and died at the age of 40. He lives on as a legendary figure in football. Bill Foulke, the football folk hero.

Frank Swift, my choice as number one goalkeeper in my old-timers' list, was a king-size personality. He deliberately turned himself into a showman because he believed that spectators deserved entertainment for their entrance money. He would pick opponents up if they dared to charge him, go down on one knee and pretend to shoot them as they approached with the ball at their feet, and he often used to kneel pleading in front of referees when decisions went against him.

Referees used to respond to his clowning with equal good humour. A rival forward threw mud in Swiftie's face during a match, and he was still wiping it out of his eyes when the ball swept past him into the net. 'But, ref,' he protested in real anger, 'I couldn't see.'

The referee, accustomed to Swift's normal humour, replied, 'Well, you'd better open your eyes, then. And wash your face before you speak to me again.'

Big Frank, who was tragically killed in the 1958 Munich air crash when travelling as a *News of the World* reporter, took only one penalty during his marvellous career with Manchester City.

This is how he recalled it in an after-dinner speech in the fifties: 'We were winning a wartime match 5–0 when we were awarded a penalty. The skipper invited me to take it. A team-mate placed the ball on the spot and I started the run-up from the edge of my own penalty area.

'I hit the ball with all my might, and it smashed into the goal with such force that it ripped a hole in the net. The ball banged into the face of an old boy standing on the terraces behind the goal, and when I went to apologise I saw that I had broken his false teeth.'

'I never had the appetite to take another penalty after that experience.'

The late, great Sam Bartram had me chuckling with this story from his days as a magnificent last line of defence for Charlton Athletic: 'I was playing on a cramped ground and could almost feel the breath of the spectators on my back. The referee made an unpopular decision and the fans pelted him with anything that was to hand. I was directly in the firing-line and had to dodge a hail of orange peel and coins. Unbeknown to me, somebody had also thrown a lighted cigarette end. It somehow got caught in the netting and set it on fire. The first I knew of it was when our trainer came dashing from the touchline and threw his bucket of water on to the fire. It was a minor cup match, and after we had won, the opposition centre-forward said, "At least we've gone out in a blaze of glory!" '

Albert Iremonger, Bill Foulke, Frank Swift and Sam Bartram – they don't make them like that any more. I make no apologies for passing on these old, old stories. It is important, in my opinion, that the younger generation realise there have been great characters in a game that is fast becoming overcrowded with faceless players. It might inspire some young players to bring personality into their game. Let's see more football played with a smile as well as style.

SAINT
5 GOLDEN OLDIES

*The days when beer was a shilling a pint, and footballers'
wages were £12 a week in the winter, and only £8 in the
summer! Ian looks back with some friends on pre- and post-
war days when the love of the game and a few laughs were
paramount.*

It's a hardy annual of a question which is
thrown at Greavsie and myself at many a
function . . . 'Don't you two wish you had been
born a little later and enjoyed all the financial
benefits present day players amass?'

There's a simple answer to that: 'Too bloody
true, mate!'

But really the sixties wasn't a bad era in
which to be a star footballer. At Liverpool
when we first started winning Leagues and
Cups we were on over a hundred quid a week
. . . not bad when you consider that the ordin-
ary working person pulled in at most twenty
quid a week for their five days' hard graft.

Jimmy, I know, got paid about the same . . .
and like me he has no real regrets. In football,
like the rest of life, there is no use wishing you
had been born in a different era. You accept
life as it comes . . . and I enjoyed every minute
of my playing career.

No. The men I feel for are not players of my
own era, but the great old boys who have
made football what it is today with their dedi-
cation, honesty and love of the game. Players
like my old boss Bill Shankly, the great Joe
Mercer, Bob Paisley, Tommy Lawton, Stan
Mortensen, Sir Stanley Matthews, Tom Finney, Len Shackleton, Jackie Milburn, big
George Young, Frank Swift, Billy Houliston,
Raich Carter and hundreds of others too
numerous to mention who were and are the
great heart of football in this country.

Many of them were playing before my time
but I've sat, listened and laughed in their
company as they regaled me long into the
night with tales of the unexpected and
talented. They were the footballers who
missed out. In the good days they got a maximum of twelve pounds a week during the football season and eight pounds in the summer.
Many of them suffered through the war and
had their careers cut tragically short because
of Hitler's madness.

Raich Carter, that wonderful inside-right
to Stanley Matthews on the England wing,
admits that he once took a job for three
pounds a week to make sure the rent and food
was paid for his family during the war years.

These lads didn't make fortunes out of football . . . but they should have. Their love of the
game has left many of them limping in pain
through their determination to play every
Saturday. Bill Shankly once told me: 'We all
loved the game, but we had families to feed
and house too. To admit an injury could mean
your first-team place . . . and remember in
those days there was always great young
talent ready to take your place. You didn't
call off unless if was an emergency.'

It wasn't all depression though. Each big
team had its class players and, as in our day
and today, laughter had its place. Shanks

Left: Bob Paisley, one of the 'great old boys who have made football what it is today'

Above: Tom Finney, in a tussle with Fulham's Quested, is another of Saint's 'golden oldies'

loved to reminisce about the good old days. His favourite player of all time was Tom Finney – the Preston Plumber. Shanks claimed that Finney 'was better than Matthews. The best player who ever graced the pitches of Britain. The man could turn you inside out like a corkscrew and then go on to score a goal. He had speed, skill and was brilliant in the box . . . a real wizard.'

I've often sat beside Tom at dinners since my old boss passed on and, as modest as ever, he would comment: 'Bill did like to exaggerate a bit, didn't he?'

From what I hear though, old Shanks wasn't going over the top about Finney's magic . . . the same tales have come at me from all quarters.

Another of my favourite 'oldies' is the great

Stan Mortensen of Blackpool and England. Stan is one of soccer's favourite characters. He has a wealth of memorable stories, and to share a glass of an evening with 'Morty' is to finish up with an aching jaw because of the laughter he evokes with his expert delivery of fabulous tales.

Stan laughs at how they call Blackpool's 4–3 victory over Bolton at Wembley 'The Matthew's Final' – so called because the whole country wanted to see Stanley (Matthews, that is) win a Cup winner's medal before he quit football.

Big Morty went down in soccer history as the first to score a hat-trick in a Wembley Cup Final that historic day . . . but it was the other Stanley who got the rave notices. The pair, of course, were big buddies both with Blackpool and England and Morty tells a wonderful story about Matthews, who was the biggest star in English football at the time. In those days, travelling back from away matches was not a quick whisk into a luxury coach with stereo, closed circuit television and videos to entertain you while you tuck into a first-class meal.

The route back to Blackpool from, say, the south coast was a long and tortuous one and almost inevitably there was a stop somewhere for a beer and a sandwich. The Saturday night stops became legendary, for Stanley (Matthews, that is) always insisted on buying the lads a drink. Most hospitable of course, but Stan was a fox off the pitch as well as on it. The coach would stop at different hostelries every away day and the reason for that was this: Matthews would move to the bar and after asking his team-mates their pleasure, would ask the landlord, 'Could you cash a cheque for a tenner?' Mine host, delighted at having the great man in his pub, would answer: 'Of course Stan – anything for you!'

Stan would duly sign the cheque and the landlord, proud as punch, would never cash it.

Instead he would have it framed and put in a place of honour in his bar . . . and Stanley would be a few quid better off and the Blackpool boys had their beer courtesy of the great man.

Morty himself was an example to everyone in football. Almost strangled by his ripcord in a parachute jump during the war, he would run through a brick wall for Blackpool and England. Yet it took years for Joe Smith, the Bloomfield Road manager, to recognise his talent. Morty once joked to me: 'He only kept me about to wash out the toilets and keep the boots clean.'

During the war Stan Mortensen also survived a horrific air crash when his plane came down in Scotland. Two of the crew lost their lives and a third his leg. Morty had severe head injuries, yet was back playing a month later. What a man!

Another great from that same era was big Frank Swift, rated amongst his peers as one of the best goalkeepers of his time. Tragically big Frank, who went on to become a sportswriter with a Manchester newspaper, died in the Munich air disaster. He was a warm, big man who, like the others of his era, would rather tell a story against himself than be embarrassed by tales of his own magnificence.

One marvellous story he used against himself was about his early days as a Manchester City keeper. A schoolboy fan approached him one day and asked him for his autograph. Frank duly signed and then the lad asked: 'How do I become as good a keeper as you?'

The big fellow replied: 'I can give you one tip. Every time I lose a goal I go home at night and draw a sketch of how I lost it. Then I can remind myself where I went wrong.'

A few weeks later City lost 8–2 in the FA

Stan Mortensen . . . one of soccer's favourite characters

56

Cup and when he came out of the players' entrance, big Frank found the same boy waiting for him. 'Another autograph?' he enquired. 'No,' said the boy, 'I'm just here to remind you you've got a lot of homework to do tonight!'

There were, of course, great players in all parts of the country after the war . . . particularly in Scotland, with great names such as George Young, Jimmy Mason, Willie Woodburn, Bobby Evans, Sammy Cox, Willie Waddell, barging Billy Houliston and the irresistible Billy Liddell, who made such an impression with my former club that they christened it 'Liddellpool'.

The dominant team in Scotland in the early post-war years was Rangers . . . and little wonder when you look at their squad . . . Jerry Dawson, George Young, Sammy Cox, Willie Thornton, Torry Gillick, Willie Woodburn and Willie Waddell – to mention but a few.

Great players all, but in their day a little 'skive' in training was accepted . . . and if you could pull one over on the trainer then so much the better. The Ibrox trainer at the time was Jimmy Smith, and he had a unique training method. Apparently Smith, in those distant days when football training consisted of lapping the park as many times as possible (preferably with not even a glimpse at a football), Smith would set a training schedule for the day, show it to the Rangers' lads . . . then set off for his trainer's room to peruse the sports pages of the *Daily Record*.

In the meantime, players such as McColl, Cox, Woodburn, Thornton and Waddell would take themselves off for a sly puff behind an Ibrox goal. Then, when enough time had lapsed, the pranksters would throw water in their faces, run the 200 yards around the pitch and report back to Jimmy puffing and panting and apparently covered in sweat.

Jimmy Smith had an eccentric way of judging if the likely lads had done their full stint.

He had a pet dog and when all had reported back he would ask the dog, 'Have they done their training then boy?' If the hound wagged its tail everything was O.K. . . . if it didn't, it was back to the training ground.

It's a good yarn, but when I watch those old Pathé movies of that great Scotland team beating England 3–1 at Wembley in 1949 with such as Young, Cox, Woodburn and Waddell running and playing their hearts out it strikes me that old Jimmy must have got wise to their ruse pretty quickly!

Sammy Cox, a peerless player in his day, returned to his beloved Scotland from his home in Canada last year and turned up again with his great friend and team-mate George Young, only a fortnight before big Corky suffered a bad stroke. In a television interview they both talked of the old times – with no regrets over money or jealousy over the lot of the player today.

But to watch the fire in Sammy's eyes, as he talked of how he gave encouragement to Billy Houliston of Queen of the South at half-time to keep up his battering-ram approach against a highly rated English team, and big George's recollection of the spirit in not only Scotland but Britain at the time, saying: 'We were just happy to be free and playing football', underlined the joy they had and continue to have in the game.

Apart from football being a much more serious affair nowadays, there are far fewer comical characters around, colourful personalities who were born to raise a laugh. Despite the image of bitterness and intense rivalry, Glasgow's Old Firm of Rangers and Celtic have had more than their fair share of happy-go-lucky jokers over the years. One of

George Young: 'We were just happy to be free and playing football'

58

the greatest wits ever to adorn a football field was Celtic inside-forward, Peter Somers, who played for Scotland four times between 1905 and 1909. A magnificent ball player with a Charlie Chaplin-like run, Peter sailed through life with laughter in his heart. One of the renowned Celtic star's contemporaries described Somers in this way: 'To try and master him in the art of back-chat was even more difficult than to deprive him of the leather once he had it under control.'

Peter Somers and Jimmy Galt, the giant Rangers and Scotland defenders, had many an epic duel during the Old Firm battles of their era, and lots of those duels were fought out with the tongue! Jimmy was a first-class golfer and enjoyed a fair measure of success in many a tournament, competing against the cream of Scotland's amateurs. During the white-hot atmosphere of a Rangers–Celtic game Peter remarked to Jimmy: 'They tell me you're a grand golfer, James.' 'Not too bad, Peter,' replied Galt. 'Well, I'll tell you what we'll do,' quipped the mischievous Somers . . . 'You teach me how to play golf and I'll teach you how to play football.'

On another occasion Somers' wit defused what appeared to be shaping up as a serious incident during a Celtic–Queen's Park game. Tom Fitchie, the famous Woolwich Arsenal, Queen's Park and Scotland forward, was inclined to lean well over the ball when he had it at his feet and, when tackled, had a habit of turning himself so that his backside prevented an opponent from getting at him . . . and it used to drive opponents wild!

During the match in question, Celtic's 'Sunny' Jim Young, failing to get near Fitchie, became more and more exasperated until, finally, he could take no more and booted the Queen's Parker on the backside. The Queen's Park supporters in the stand rose to their feet, howling 'Get him off the park!' (Or words to that effect.) The referee ran towards Young and Fitchie and it looked as though the Celt was sure to receive his marching orders. The ever-alert Somers shuffled over, arriving on the scene at the same time as the official. 'Look here, Fitchie, old son, play the game,' said Somers in a voice full of reproach. A look of utter astonishment crossed the Queen's Park man's face. 'What do you mean? Am I not playing the game?' he demanded. 'I'll show you what I mean,' replied Peter, and grinning broadly at the referee, he placed the ball at his feet and proceeded with his Chaplin-like action to dribble the ball about twenty yards and back again. Fitchie roared with laughter, Young laughed . . . the referee laughed, while the crowd wondered what on earth was going on. The game then restarted with Jim Young still on the field.

Almost every youngster who arrived at Ibrox between 1906 and the outbreak of the Great War in 1914 had to 'run the gauntlet' of the dapper Jimmy Galt's incomparable wit. The Rangers star was one of the cheekiest practical jokers in the history of the sport. Seated beside a young player following a pre-match meal, Jimmy would place a florin ostentatiously under the plate as a tip for the waiter and, in nine cases out of ten, the new arrival would do likewise. However, before rising from the table, Galt, when nobody was looking, would slip the two shilling piece back into his pocket.

On one occasion Jimmy decided to raise the gratuity to the sizeable sum of five shillings and made certain that the newcomer saw him place two half-crowns under the plate. 'The usual tip by any Rangers player,' he said to his youthful club-mate who, rather than let the famous Glasgow Rangers down, dug deeply into his wage packet and followed suit with five shillings.

Minutes later, the Rangers party left. About an hour afterwards Jimmy Galt's face suddenly turned a whiter shade of pale. 'Good God,' he blurted out, 'I forgot to take my five bob back!' Needless to say, that costly lapse of memory put an end to the tipping joke!

Throughout the years, many comical characters have thrilled the crowds at soccer stadiums up and down the United Kingdom. But perhaps the greatest character of them all was the incomparable Len Shackleton, whose antics during his playing days with Sunderland and England not only kept the crowds amused, but frequently landed him in 'hot water' with the authorities. Dubbed 'The Clown Prince of Soccer', Len was a complete extrovert, a fun-loving exhibitionist who could do virtually anything with the ball . . . some say he could even make it talk!

Always at least a move ahead of the players around him, 'Shack' was one of a select few who can truly be termed a footballing genius. He was a sheer artist, one of the greatest and most colourful characters ever to don a football jersey and to display his skills on the soccer field. How the Sunderland fans on those famous terraces at Roker Park adored their incurable joker!

Once when Len was playing against a continental side, he got exasperated by a defender who tugged at his shorts every time he went near him. When he could take it no longer, Shack took off his shorts, handed them to the opponent and said: 'There you are, if you like them so much you can keep them!'

Many considered his approach to the game to be far too jocular and carefree which, no doubt, explains why he made only five full international appearances for England when there were few, if any, who could begin to match his skills as an inside-forward. Superbly balanced, Shackleton took great delight in tormenting even the greatest of defenders, turning them this way and that with sheer artistry and bewildering ball control, until they were so dizzy they couldn't even remember which day of the week it was. How Arsenal must have rued the day they rejected Len when he was only a slip of a lad, considering him far too frail to have any chance of making the grade in the strength-sapping, white-hot atmosphere of the First Division.

When asked to name the players he most admired throughout his years of watching and being involved in football, Jim Finney, that renowned English referee, put Shackleton at the very top of his list: 'My most vivid recollection of the great man came when I was a spectator at St Andrews, Birmingham,' said Finney. 'Shackleton had a field day, teasing and tormenting their defenders with his skills. One incident stands out clearly. Collecting the ball on the wing, he set off on a run and, as he saw the full-back rushing in to challenge, coolly slipped it inside and past him. There was no way of avoiding a collision with the unfortunate fellow who had committed himself so badly ... so Shack simply nipped off the field, jinked around the linesman and then returned to collect the ball and continue his route to goal. The crowd were in hysterics and Shackleton's face was the picture of innocence when the referee penalised his impudence.'

That incident was typical of the peerless Len Shackleton, an extrovert soccer genius whose charismatic personality won over the hearts and minds of soccer fans wherever he played ... a fact which would be readily sub-stantiated by those fortunate enough to have witnessed his breathtaking play, as well as by the luckless opponents who he mesmerised. No, there was never a dull moment when the incomparable Mr Shackleton was around!

There was no finer post-war half-back than that delectable Irishman, Danny Blanchflower. In the course of an illustrious career with Aston Villa, Tottenham Hotspur and Northern Ireland, there were very few on the soccer field who posed many problems for 'Danny Boy'.

Stanley Matthews I've touched on already, but his name could strike fear into the most formidable of defenders. Yes, the 'Wizard of the Dribble' was as slippery as an eel, a real bundle of tricks who was almost impossible to contain. Great though Blanchflower was, even he found it an awesome experience to play against the Blackpool winger, as the talented Irishman delightfully recalled in the *Danny Blanchflower Soccer Book:*

'You may have your own plan on how to stop him ... but so has your manager, coach, and all your team-mates. And being on your side, they are awfully anxious to give you the benefit of their advice. "Make him do this," says one. "Make him do that," says another. "Stay close to him ... Keep away from him ... Watch him ... Ignore him," ... it goes on; and when you leave that meeting your head is buzzing as if you had been hit with a goalpost.

'Finally you get out there and the phantom with the number seven on his back gets the ball. Unlike most other players he does not try to avoid you; comes wriggling his casual way towards you. You tense yourself and watch the ball. Now he's within your reach and he sways outwards to his right, like a snake. He's going down the wing, you think, and lunge forward with your left foot to block

Danny Blanchflower found Stanley Matthews almost impossible to contain

62

the ball. All of a sudden ... Whsst! ... this blur goes past you on the inside and your eyes pop up in amazement.

'... He's got the ball again ... but this time you are ready for him. He's not going to get away with that again. So, as he sways leisurely outwards to his right again, you tackle forward, this time with your right foot to stop him coming inside and ... Whsst! ... the blur goes past you on the outside ... Next time round you are more careful, but ... Whsst! ... He's much too fast and you are chasing that blur again ... Then ... Whsst! ... there he goes again, and you are lying on the ground and saying to yourself: "To hell with it. I've had enough of this fellow."'

Football, more than any other sport or entertainment, is, and always has been, littered with characters who, had they opted for a career on the stage, would have been an instant hit in the glare of the footlights from Southampton to Aberdeen. Characters like the afore-mentioned Peter Somers, Jimmy Galt and Len Shackleton, men who were the footballing equivalents of Charlie Chaplin, Tony Hancock and Benny Hill.

Sandy McNab of Sunderland, West Bromwich Albion and Scotland fame was another likely lad who always had an impish smile on his face. An outstanding half-back in the immediate pre-war seasons, the Glasgow man was an ardent fan of Glasgow Rangers and any Ibrox player who found himself in the company of Sandy had to endure an almost steady gaze of adulation. During Scotland's Central European tour of 1937, Sandy played in the left-half position for his country against Austria in Vienna. A week later that same left-half berth was occupied by the legendary Rangers star, George Brown, when the Scots faced Czechoslovakia in Prague. Scotland won 3–1 in the first international fixture between the nations and Brown formed part of a really brilliant triangle; the others being Rangers Bob McPhail and former Ibrox star Torry Gillick, who was then playing with Everton. Seated in the stand, Sandy McNab was thrilled to see his Rangers' hero, George Brown, playing such a magnificent role in Scotland's victory. 'Look at Geordie,' McNab roared aloud, in a voice full of delight. 'Just look at him ... look at his passing, look at his positional play, look at his covering up. Imagine me being preferred to the likes of Geordie. Those crazy selectors must be totally off their rockers!'

There always have been laughs in football and there always will be ... it's that kind of game! A game which can so easily become an obsession rather than simply a sport or a hobby.

In conclusion, some pertinent words from the much-loved Joe Mercer, that most respected of English players and managers, who, after being sacked by Aston Villa and spending fourteen worrying months on the soccer sidelines, took over the managerial reins at Manchester City and summed up his burning passion for the game with these words: 'Football can live without me, but I can't live without football.'

Not a bad epitaph I reckon for all of those Golden Oldies who have helped make football our national game.

Saint and Greavsie's

WORLD CUP SPY MISSION

WRITTEN AND ILLUSTRATED BY BARRY ROBERTS.

TEE HEE HEE... I KNOW IT DAVID... I DOOO!! HEE HEE .. TEE HEE!!

FORGET IT JIM. DOESN'T MATTER HOW MUCH YOU PRACTISE.. YOU'LL NEVER BE AS POPULAR AS EMLYN HUGHES. ANYWAY.. WE'VE JUST RECEIVED A SUMMONS.

I'VE ALREADY PAID THAT SPEEDING FINE!!

NOT THAT KIND OF SUMMONS! THIS ONE'S FROM THE PRIME MINISTER HERSELF! SHE AND DENIS NEED OUR HELP. A BIG OVERSEAS JOB.

DON'T TELL ME MARK'S GOT HIMSELF LOST AGAIN!

THEY ARRIVE AT NUMBER TEN

BLIMEY! WHAT'S TERRY VENABLES DOING AT NUMBER ELEVEN?

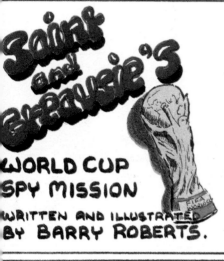

ADVISING ON THE BALANCE OF PAYMENTS. HE'S THE ONLY ONE WHO'S SPENT MORE THAN THE CHANCELLOR THIS YEAR!

AH.. SAINT AND GREAVSIE. YOU'RE NO DOUBT AWARE OF THE FORTH-COMING WORLD CUP. WELL.. I'M AFRAID THE ENGLAND TEAM ARE IN DESPERATE NEED OF YOUR SERVICES.. AND TELL MR SAINT JOHN HE MAY STOP BOWING.

WE COULDN'T PLAY.. WE'RE TOO OLD SIR. NOT ONLY THAT.. I DIDN'T EVEN GET A GAME IN THE 1966 FINAL!!

NOT TO PLAY IN YOU SILLY MAN!! IT'S A SECRET MISSION TO OBTAIN FACTS ON OUR OPPONENTS. YOU WILL VISIT ALL COUNTRIES WHO HOPE TO BE THERE, INCLUDING THE HOST NATION, ITALY.

ITALY! AGGH! I'D RATHER SHARE A DESERT ISLAND WITH EMLYN HUGHES! ANYWAY.. THEY'LL REMEMBER ME.

ACCORDING TO MY INFORMATION, NO-BODY CAN REMEMBER **THAT** FAR BACK.. UNLESS YOU'RE AN ELEPHANT. NOW TAKE THIS LETTER TO THE FOREIGN OFFICE AND SEND MR ROBSON IN ON YOUR WAY OUT. I'VE A PROPOSITION TO MAKE HIM.

A KNIGHTHOOD IF HE WINS?

WORSE! A SEASON TICKET FOR MANCHESTER UNITED IF HE **DOESN'T**!!

I WOULDN'T LIKE TO BE IN BOBBY ROBSON'S SHOES.

NOR ME. NOT WITH THAT THREAT OF A SEASON TICKET IF I LOST!!

MOVE ALONG NOW PLEASE

AT THE AIRPORT

THESE BUSKERS ARE EVERYWHERE, JIM.

IM LEANING ON THE LAMPOSTAT...

TA: GUV'NOR

I KNOW.. YOU'D THINK BRIAN MOORE WOULD HAVE ENOUGH MONEY. HERE, GIVE HIM THIS 50 PEE...

THEY LAND AT BERMUDA

BUT BERMUDA AREN'T IN THE WORLD CUP, GREAVSIE.

I KNOW. BUT WHO WANTS TO VISIT RUSSIA AT THIS TIME OF YEAR!

AH.. THIS IS THE LIFE, SAINT. LAZY DAYS IN THE SUN, SIPPING COOL DRINKS. SO THIS IS WHAT IT'S LIKE TO BE RON ATKINSON.

ATCKO'S NOT LAID ON A BEACH SINCE THAT TIME GREEN-PEACE SAVE THE WHALE DRAGGED HIM BACK IN THE WATER. COME ON, TIME WE LEFT... NEXT STOP FRANCE.

FRANCE

'OW ABOUT ZE DISGUISE? I WEEL SAY ZIS ONLY ONCE. EVER SEEN FROGS LEGS, SAINT?

YEH, TOMMY SMITH HAD A PAIR BELONGING TO A FRENCH WINGER!

NOTRE DAME. QUASIMODO LIVED UP THERE.

THAT NAME RINGS A BELL, SAINT. AND TALKING OF QUASIMODO... I MUST SEND GARY NEWBON A POSTCARD.

THEY SPY ON A FRENCH TRAINING SESSION

HOW CAN THEY GET FIT SITTING IN A CAFÉ ALL DAY?

THEY DON'T NEED TO GET FIT JIM. THEY'VE EATEN SO MUCH GARLIC THAT THE ENGLISH DEFENDERS WON'T GET WITHIN 100 YARDS OF THEM!!

NEXT STOP GERMANY.

I STILL SAY YOU LOOK LIKE A LAGER ADVERT!! LET'S HAVE A SCOUT AROUND.

BORUSSIA MOENCHENGLADBACH FOOTENBALL CLUB

GUESS WHO'S THE MOST UNPOPULAR SUPPORTER IN THIS PLACE?

WHO?

THE ONE WHO SHOUTS "GIVE US A 'B'"!!!

THE GERMANS PREPARE IN SECRET

CAREFUL NOW. THE LAST TIME WE LOOKED OVER THE WRONG GERMAN WALL WE GOT SHOT AT!!! CAN YOU SEE ANYTHING?

YEH.. THEY'RE PRACTISING SET PIECES. THEIR NUMBER EIGHT LOOKS LIKE HE CAN THUMP THE BALL.

TWACK

HE'S PRETTY ACCURATE TOO!!

FANCY A ROUND OF GOLF WHILE WE'RE IN SPAIN, JIM? WHAT'S YOUR HANDICAP THESE DAYS?

STILL 'SPORTING TRIANGLES', SAINT!!

WE'LL GET SOME INFORMATION FROM JOHN TOSHACK. DID YOU KNOW HE SPEAKS FLUENT SPANISH?

SPANISH! HA.. I'VE YET TO HEAR HIM SPEAK FLUENT ENGLISH. HURRY UP SAINT.. WE'VE ONLY GOT A WEEK.

EVER BEEN TO ONE OF THOSE BLOOD SPORTS?

EL TORRO
MANUEL LABOUR
QUATTRO TORROS

YEH.. A COUPLE OF YEARS AGO WHEN I SAW URUGUAY PLAY!!

BACK AT THE HOTEL

SENORS... AN URGENT MESSAGE FROM LONDON. ZEY WANT YOU TO FLY TO RUSSIA PRONTO!

DIDN'T EVEN HAVE TIME FOR A SUNTAN. RUSSIA EH?? FANCY A VISIT TO THE URALS, SAINT?

NO THANKS. I WENT AT THE AIRPORT BEFORE WE TOOK OFF.

RED SQUARE

LET'S SEE.. WHERE'S THAT RUSSIAN TRAINING CAMP?

ON THE OUTSKIRTS OF MOSCOW IF YOU'RE PLAYING WELL.

AND WHAT IF YOU'RE NOT PLAYING WELL?

SIBERIA! LOOK.. IT SAYS HERE THAT THE KREMLIN F.C. PLAYED THE SECRET POLICE LAST NIGHT.

WHAT WAS THE SCORE?

I DON'T KNOW.. THEY WOULDN'T TELL ANYONE. CAN'T SEE MUCH ABOUT THE WORLD CUP IN THIS SPORTS SECTION.

A STRANGER APPROACHES

HEY COMRADES.. IT'S SAINT AND GREAVSKI.. VE HEAR ALL LATEST NEWS IN RUSSIA OF YOUR WORLD CUPSKI SQUAD FOR ITALY. BOBBY MOORE.. NOBBY STILES. VE READ IT IN ZE BLACK MARKET NEWS PAPERS.

BLIMEY! THEY MUST GET THE 'SUN' OVER HERE! I BET THEY THINK STAN MATTHEWS STILL PLAYS.

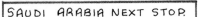

SUDDENLY THE CROWD ROARS

HEY!! WHO'SA DAT NEXT TO BRIAN CLOUGH

BLIMEY! I HEARD CLOUGHIE WAS AFTER A JOB IN ITALY.. BUT NOT THIS ONE!!

PASSING THE COLOSSEUM

DIDN'T KNOW MILLWALL HAD BEEN PLAYING HERE? WHERE TO NOW ELTON?

WINDSOR CASTLE. BY THE WAY, DID YOU KNOW I'VE WON THE SPORTS PERSONALITY OF THE YEAR AWARD?

WINDSOR CASTLE

FOR YOUR SERVICES TO THE WORLD CUP SQUAD...

ARISE SIR SAINT AND SIR GREAVSIE, SIR SAINT?? ARE YOU ALRIGHT??

SIR SAINT?? SIR SAINT SIR SAINT SIRS??

YOU ALRIGHT SAINT?

WHAT HAPPENED JIM?

YOU'VE GOT SUNSTROKE.

I MUST HAVE. I DREAMED WE'D BEEN KNIGHTED... CLOUGHIE WAS POPE... AND ELTON WELSBY WAS THE SPORTS PERSONALITY OF THE YEAR

DON'T KNOW ABOUT PASSING OUT? YOU MUST HAVE BEEN DELIRIOUS TO BELIEVE THAT!

I SUPPOSE THE IDEA OF US BEING KNIGHTED TAKES SOME BELIEVING.

NO, NO.. I COULD BELIEVE THAT.. BUT AS FOR ELTON WINNING SPORTS PERSONALITY!! WELL.. WE'D BETTER GET GOING. MARK THATCHER'S HERE IN HIS RALLY CAR TO GIVE US A LIFT HOME.

HAW HAW

I DIDN'T KNOW SAUDI WERE HAVING A RALLY?

THEY'RE NOT.. LUCKILY FOR US, HE WAS ON HIS WAY TO MEXICO AND HAD THE ROAD MAP UPSIDE DOWN. LEFT AT THE NEXT CAMEL, MARK.

THE END

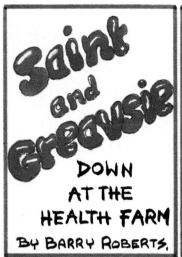

Saint and Greavsie

DOWN AT THE HEALTH FARM

BY BARRY ROBERTS.

SAINT AND GREAVSIE ENDURE YET ANOTHER STUDIO LUNCH.

PHEW!! IF I EAT ANY MORE LOBSTER SAINT, I MIGHT END UP LOOKING LIKE ONE!

WHAT DO YOU MEAN MIGHT!!

MORE CAVIAR ANYONE?

COME ON JIM. WE'VE GOT THE ANNUAL CHECK UP WITH THE STUDIO DOCTOR IN 5 MINUTES! CAN'T YOU GET UP THOSE STAIRS ANY FASTER?

ONLY IF I TAKE THE LIFT. SAINT. I HAVEN'T FELT THIS TIRED SINCE I CARRIED DICKIE DAVIES' WAGE PACKET UP TO HIS OFFICE!

PUFF! PANT!

YOU'RE NOT FIT ENOUGH GREAVSIE. ACCORDING TO MY HEIGHT AND WEIGHT CHART, YOU SHOULD BE EIGHT FEET TALL!! WHAT'S THE LIGHTEST YOU'VE WEIGHED?

7 POUNDS 8 OUNCES DOC. MIND YOU... THAT WAS IN 1939!!

SIMPLE SOLUTION. ALL REPORTERS WILL SPEND A WEEK AT A HEALTH FARM. REG GUTTERIDGE HAS JUST COMPLETED HIS AND SHOULD BE OUT OF INTENSIVE CARE SOON. MEANWHILE, GREAVSIE CAN START BY JOGGING 5 MILES A DAY!

GREAVSIE JOGGING!! BETTER PEOPLE HAVE TRIED AND FAILED DOC! NAMELY SPURS, INTER MILAN AND ALF RAMSEY WHEN HE MANAGED ENGLAND!!

5 MILES A DAY BLIMEY, AFTER 3 MONTHS I COULD END UP BACK AT CENTRAL T.V. IN BIRMINGHAM!

BARBED WIRE SAINT? WHO'S GOING TO BREAK INTO THIS PLACE?

HEALTH FARM
SPECIAL DISCOUNTS FOR TV. EXECUTIVES. NO JOB TOO BIG!!

IT'S THERE TO STOP US FROM BREAKING OUT, JIM. COME ON, LET'S GET INSIDE

HELLO MISTERS SAINT AND GREAVSIE. MY NAME IS HELGA. I AM YOUR COACH AND I VILL KNOCK YOU INTO SHAPE!

DES LYNHAM SUPERSTAR

BOB WILSON FRIEND OF DES LYN

SHE MAKES FATIMA WHITBREAD LOOK LIKE WILLY CARSON! SHE'S GOT MUSCLES IN PLACES I HAVEN'T EVEN GOT PLACES!!

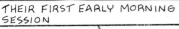

LUNCH LATER THAT DAY
A PIECE OF LETTUCE AND A GLASS OF WATER? LAST TIME I HAD THIS WAS WHEN YOU PAID FOR LUNCH, SAINT.

I THINK IT'S TIME WE SPOKE TO THE MANAGER.

TOMMY DOCHERTY!! YOU'RE THE MANAGER?

THAT'S RIGHT BOYS. WHAT WAS IT YOU WANTED?

IT'S A WASTE OF TIME COMPLAINING TO THE DOC, SAINT. ON HIS RECORD HE'LL PROBABLY BE SACKED NEXT WEEK!!

THAT'S IT JIM. IT'S OVER THE WALL AT MIDNIGHT. ALL WE'VE GOT TO FIND IS A LADDER.

MANAGER WANTED

WHO NEEDS A LADDER WHEN WE CAN STAND ON MARTIN TYLER'S SHOULDERS

THEY MAKE THEIR ESCAPE

A FULL MOON JIM.

YEH, ALAN PARRY SHOULD BE BOUNCING OFF THE WALLS TONIGHT. HEY MARTIN... WATCH WHERE YOU'RE PUTTING YOUR... AGGGGHH!!!

WE'LL HAVE TO THINK OF AN EXCUSE TO TELL THE BOSS WHEN WE GET BACK.

PSSSSSSST

THERE'S ONLY ONE EXCUSE HE'S GUARANTEED TO BELIEVE. WE SAY WE HAD LUNCH WITH RON ATKINSON AND PUT ALL THE WEIGHT BACK ON. HEY!!! WHAT'S THAT NOISE? ARE YOU HISSING, SAINT?

NO, IT'S SWEAT! OH NO! WE'VE GOT A PUNCTURE!!

WE'LL HAVE TO WALK IT THEN. IF WE DON'T GET BACK FOR SATURDAY'S SHOW WE'RE IN TROUBLE.

YOU'RE TWO HOURS LATE! I HOPE YOU REALIZE THAT THE 'SAINT AND GREAVSIE' SHOW'S FINISHED!

LWT

THE 'NEWS OF THE WORLD' HAVE BEEN SAYING THAT FOR YEARS, BOSS.

I MEANT THE SHOW HAS ALREADY GONE OUT! LUCKILY, WE HAD TWO EXCELLENT REPLACEMENTS WHO DID THE JOB EVEN BETTER THAN YOU!! WE'VE ALSO HAD HUNDREDS OF CALLS FROM VIEWERS SAYING HOW MUCH FITTER YOU LOOKED.

I DON'T UNDERSTAND. WHO COULD POSSIBLY DO A BETTER JOB THAN THE SAINT AND ME??

YOUR 'SPITTING IMAGE' PUPPETS, OF COURSE!!

FOOTBALL'S A FUNNY OLD GAME.

HA HA HA HA YOU KILL ME GREAVSIE!

THE END

6 THE TRIALS OF TELEVISION

Greavsie this year celebrated ten years in television – and in the following pages, he remembers some of the famous personalities he has met and suffered with! As a have-a-go sports expert with Central Television, Jimmy has had his moments, some of them hair-raising as well as hilarious.

These days the whole world recognises Eddie 'The Eagle' Edwards as Britain's most popular sporting failure. Finishing last in the Olympic ski-jump – an event where finishing in one piece is, I admit, a triumph – has made Eddie our unlikeliest sporting hero.

What most of the world doesn't know is that I discovered Eddie's knack for sporting disasters four years earlier. On my television beat for Central Television, I was intrigued watching a feature on this crazy bloke from Cheltenham trying to break the world speed record while locked into skis on top of a car. I have to say it was a world record with which I was not familiar. But there he was, Eddie Edwards, plasterer by trade, whizzing along on top of a souped-up car in this weird spaceman's helmet trying to reach a new world record speed of 143 miles per hour.

The scene was a disused and deserted airfield in Gloucestershire – and that's where my first glimpse of Eddie's appetite for spectacular failure took place. As the car's speedometer crept towards 140 miles an hour and Eddie was in sight of the record, guess what happened. He ran out of road! As they hurtled towards the end of the runway and a nasty-looking bramble hedge, the brakes went on and Eddie had blown it.

But as we all know now, Eddie is nothing if not a trier. Within a couple of weeks, he was on the phone to Central's Sports Editor, Jeff Farmer, saying he was ready to make another attempt and he had arranged to use an unopened section of the M42 in Warwickshire to make sure he had enough road. And could Greavsie come along to verify the record?

Farmer, who had narrowly failed to dispose of me on a hang-glider a few months earlier, said that not only would Greavsie come along, he would also make an attempt on the record himself.

So at the crack of dawn a few days later, we assembled, Farmer and me, director Stuart Wilson, a video crew and a police escort – and, of course, Eddie, complete with skis and his spaceman's helmet, specially designed to cut through wind resistance.

Eddie was confident. The road was wide, smooth and certainly long enough at over three miles. This was going to be his first step towards fame.

Three hours and several increasingly embarrassing phone calls later, we were all

McCall's last minute equalizer for Everton in the
FA Cup Final . . .

Below: The Anfield goal after the tragedy of
Hillsborough

. . . but Ian Rush scores the winner in extra time.
Final score 3–2 to Liverpool

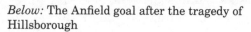

Chris Woods tips the ball over in the Scottish Cup
Final . . .

. . . and Rangers' Davie Cooper is determined to
beat Roy Aitken to the ball . . .

. . . but Celtic won the cup! Final score at Hampden,
1–0 to Celtic

still standing on the hard shoulder. Eddie's car had not turned up – he had booked it for the wrong day. The mission was aborted and the apologetic Eddie announced that his pursuit of that particular record was finished.

'What's your next project, then, Eddie?' I asked.

'Greavsie, you are not going to believe this, but I have just started training for the Winter Olympics in 1988. I intend to represent Great Britain in the ski-jump,' said Eddie.

'Are you sure? Have you tried it?'

'Not yet – but I'll be there in Calgary, mark my words.'

He sure was, in all his bespectacled glory, and whatever the Olympic purists might say, you have to admire the man's courage.

Having been in on the start of Eddie's long record of failures, I have to admit that I have also been on the receiving end of one of his rare victories. When I learned that Eddie had been booked to appear in the third series of *Sporting Triangles,* I thought I would be lumbered with him again. Not so – I was delighted to discover he was partnering Emlyn Hughes.

Inevitably, Eddie knew next to nothing about his specialist sport of skiing. I think he answered 'Zurbriggen' to every question, so had to get one right. But somehow he finished up on the winning team. I'm still trying to work that one out.

One final thought on Eddie the Eagle. His next ambition, I'm told, is to appear on that television commercial where the guy swings across the skyscrapers on a rope and lands in his bird's boudoir with a box of Cadbury's Milk Tray. If that's the next time you see Eddie, remember you read it here first.

Eddie is certainly the most unusual sporting personality I have met on my television travels. But there have been some other interesting journeys – like on the back of Barry Sheene's motorbike. No problem, Greavsie,

they said. Just turn up at the Donington circuit in Leicestershire, put on some leathers and a crash helmet and Barry will take you round the track on his pillion.

So they stuck a microphone on me, Barry opened up the throttle and away we went. Even when we touched 100 miles per hour, it was no sweat. We had a clear track in front of us and as I gave my running commentary, I was becoming a bit flash about it all.

Then as we swept past the pits, out came twenty riders who had decided to pull a fast one on Barry and me – and provide a taste of what it's really like in a bike race.

Barry responded by showing them that world champions cannot be buzzed. And there I was, rigid on the pillion clinging to Barry and shouting: 'What are these maniacs doing on our track?'

Although Barry managed to get me round in one piece, all I can say is that it's a good job I was wearing leather trousers.

By the way, Barry is one of the nicest guys I have ever come across in sport. A chirpy Londoner, he has that never-say-die attitude which personifies great champions – no matter what sport they are in. He used to joke that his legs were like a Meccano set – they had been smashed and pinned together with metal studs so often by doctors following several major bike crashes. Yet he always came up smiling and he didn't dwell on the bad days – only on the good ones. And of course the laughs he had during a great career as world champion. He has now emigrated to Australia and I know Oz will be the better for his presence.

Mind you, I needed a suit of armour when I played John McEnroe at tennis. He had been helicoptered from London to the indoor tennis centre at Telford and he's about as keen on that form of travel as I am.

We had a quiet chat over beans on toast and

I was surprised to find he was a keen soccer fan and had a reputation in New York as a slippery left-winger. When we went on court I discovered just how hard a top professional tennis player hits the ball. 'Don't ease up,' I suggested to McEnroe for the sake of our game looking real for the cameras. He didn't.

I didn't even see his first service, let alone get a racket to it. There was a dull thud as the ball hit the back of the court. It was all I could do to keep out of harm's way and even when McEnroe slipped down a few gears to dolly drops, I just managed to lose our one-set match 6–0!

It was amazing to watch Stefan Edberg handle McEnroe at the 1989 Wimbledon Championships. Having faced 'Superbrat', I would not have put money on anyone being able to destroy him three sets to love, yet the Swede did exactly that. How he ever returned those services I'll never know.

And it seems tennis is a funny old game too – for what did Boris Becker do to Edberg in the final – beat him three sets to love. Big Boris, they say, has the hardest service on grass – he certainly blitzed Stefan off the court.

Me? I'm just glad that it was McEnroe I faced up to and not those bombs of Boris. I reckon if I ever came up against that young German I'd come off the court a hunchback!

Another keen soccer fan from another part of sport I have been privileged to meet is one of the world's top golfers, Seve Ballesteros.

Seve is a Barcelona fanatic and his knowledge of football is impressive. He even remembers the 1966 World Cup – which is almost more than I can say.

I took up golf again recently after a gap of ten years, and it's only when you play regularly and watch the likes of Seve you realise how big the gap is between amateur and professional golf. I struggle to hit the ball 200 yards putting the full Greavsie weight behind the swing ... and that's not inconsiderable as Saint keeps reminding me.

Seve, during our clinic, hit the ball one-handed, on one leg and could juggle it as well as any Palladium act on the end of his wedge. As a kid, he learned his golf using only a three-iron for every shot – including bunker shots. Quite amazing!

During our interview, I asked him, 'How do I get stop on my three-iron shots?' Seve answered: 'How far do you hit your three-iron?' 'About 150 yards,' I replied. Seve retorted: 'Mama mia – just what do you want stop on it for?!'

Mind you, I do have one golfing edge over Seve – I also hit my putts 150 yards!

Seve played nine holes for the cameras at La Manga in Spain and proved that he is not just a fabulous golfer, but also a great entertainer. He does everything with a golfball except make it talk and I could only stand in amazement when his virtuoso performance of trick shots was climaxed by hitting a driver over 200 yards while on his knees.

7 A MANAGER'S LOT!

Who'd be a manager? Every year come the inevitable sackings as Boards around the country decide that it's the boss's fault that teams are not as successful as they would wish them to be. Yet still the former greats of the game queue up to take their chance on the managerial merry-go-round . . . everyone hoping that he has the Midas touch needed to set a club alight. It has been described as the worst job in the world but hand in hand with the lack of security goes the laughter, and in this chapter Ian and Jimmy look back on some great characters and some magical stories of the men in charge . . . starting with some reminiscing by Saint.

Saint

In previous books I have talked about my own experiences under the greatest character of all . . . my old guv'nor Bill Shankly. Shanks was a one-off, an unconscious comedian whose love of football was so serious it became funny to all around him, and the stories of my old Liverpool boss have been well documented in our two previous tomes.

All of Liverpool cried when Shanks died. He was, like myself, from north of the border, but he epitomised Liverpool in the sixties – brash, breezy, and with a rough warmth which marked him out as special to red and blue alike.

When a young reporter asked Shanks if he looked on football as 'A matter of life or death,' the old feller growled: 'Son, it's much more important than that.' That line has become part of football legend. But really it's worth repeating for Shanks might have been etching an epitaph for life as a football manager.

I know . . . I've been there with Motherwell and Portsmouth and I know that every club manager lives and dies a hundred times through any Saturday match.

But while every boss lives one step away from the dole queue, the love of the game sees players queuing up each season hoping for room at the top for them. I can promise them two things: heartaches . . . and a load of laughs!

I've been lucky enough to be with people who are not only great managers but also great characters, and some of the fun I've had over the years will send me laughing to my grave.

After leaving Portsmouth, I went back into football with big Jack Charlton at Sheffield Wednesday and I've touched already on some of my days at Hillsborough in Yorkshire Tykes.

Now Jack, it has to be said, has one of the finest football minds around. He has been a success at every club he's managed and has

'Forgetful' Jack Charlton remembers the one that got away

now achieved the impossible . . . an Englishman revered in the Republic of Ireland . . . following that country's great run in international competition.

It doesn't surprise me that Jack has had great success as the Republic supremo. The big fellow would be a success in any manager's job . . . he knows the strengths and capabilities of players and uses them to the full. Also, he has one of the best assistants in the business alongside him in Maurice Setters, the former Manchester United wing-half and skipper. Maurice and I were Jack's coaches at

Sheffield Wednesday and many a laugh we had too.

Now it's no secret that Jack, while he has one of the finest football brains in the game, is also a little, shall we say, forgetful!

They say an elephant never forgets, well Jack was known as the giraffe because of his long neck . . . and he forgot everything. I remember boarding the team coach for an away game one morning and asking him where we

73

were stopping for lunch. Jack had forgotten to book anywhere. 'Tell the driver to find somewhere,' he retorted . . . not an easy task with a coachload of hungry footballers.

Jack actually once left two players behind at a hotel when Wednesday set off for an FA Cup semi-final. The two lads had to get a taxi to the game!

Mind you, on one occasion his loss of memory probably saved Maurice Setters and myself a few quid. One night after a reserve match at Hillsborough, a Wednesday director invited Setters and myself into the boardroom for a drink. As the beer flowed time passed quickly and suddenly Maurice and I were last to leave the ground.

When I tried to get back into the boot room for my jacket and house keys, the groundsman had already locked up and left for the night . . . and Maurice and I were stranded.

Setters, as anyone who played against him in the sixties would vouch, could tackle his way through a barn door, never mind a bootroom door. The door gave way to his boot and we had our keys. But Jack was fuming in the morning. One of the big man's qualities as a manager is that he believes in standards, and the next day he let us know in no uncertain terms that he expected us to set examples for players, not resort to what he called 'horseplay'. He wanted to take the cost of a new door out of our wages but Maurice pleaded innocence just as he did in his playing days and we got away with it. Mind you we never crossed the big man again!

It's fairly well known that big Jack does like a bit of hunting, shooting and fishing and one night, after one of his famous 'scouting trips' to Scotland, he returned to Hillsborough for a midweek match. He arrived in the dressing room just in time to find Tony Toms, our trainer, filling his bag with bandages and sprays in preparation for the game.

'Tomsy,' said Jack, 'get the lads in here . . . I want a word with them before the game.'

Tomsy looked at him open-mouthed. 'What do you mean, boss? They've just kicked off!'

Big Jack shrugged his shoulders, mumbled something about thinking it was a 7.45 kickoff, then walked to the dug-out!

Unorthodox is what big Jack is . . . brilliantly unorthodox a lot of the time. I'll never forget his first training session at Wednesday. The players were out with Maurice and myself doing some warming-up exercises when he strolled out into the centre circle, carrying a mug of tea and smoking a fag while talking tactics.

Names were his greatest failing. Maurice and I had to prompt him when he was running through his team selection. He'd point at a player and say, 'I want you to mark their centre-forward er . . . er . . . er . . .' and Maurice or I would whisper, 'Mark Smith, boss.'

Former Liverpool star Craig Johnston, who was under Jack at Middlesbrough, told me he had the same problem there. In fact he used to pin up the teamsheet at 'Boro and put 'Kangaroo' instead of Johnston. At least it had registered that Craig was an Aussie . . . I just wonder how big Jack copes in Dublin!

Over the years Jack has been a popular choice for football programmes on television. He doesn't pull his punches and will let rip with honest opinions about anything in the game . . . at times leaving soccer's top brass wincing with his criticisms. But his problems with names have had us all giggling behind the scenes. He once baffled a TV interviewer by referring to the great Brazilian 'Peel'. We think he meant Pele!

And during the 1982 World Cup Finals in Spain another great Brazilian Socrates was tagged 'So-crates', as in milk bottles, by the big man. What would the great philosopher himself have thought of that one!

I wonder how big Jack would have handled the situation which confronted a referee during a Huddersfield Town match back in the seventies. The Huddersfield winger had made a couple of dubious tackles during the game and when he made a third the man in black dashed across to him, brandishing notebook and pencil. 'That's once too often, son,' he claimed. 'What's your name?'

'Dick Krzywicki,' replied the player.

'Well, don't do it again,' mumbled the referee, diplomatically putting the notebook back in his pocket.

Big Jack would have been well worth hearing on Mr Kryzwicki, I'm sure.

Many a laugh we had over Jack's little name problem ... and none bigger than on the night we played Aston Villa in a midweek League Cup-tie. We stopped for our usual tea and toast at a hotel *en route* and the big fellow duly went through his team talk in his own uniquely confusing manner. When the meeting broke up, our striker Rodger Wylde came to me and asked if he was playing. 'Didn't the boss read your name out?' I asked. 'Yes,' said Rodger, 'but he named two other forwards too and there seemed to be twelve players in his side,' answered the confused Wylde.

I immediately called Jack over and diplomatically enquired: 'Rodger here isn't quite sure what you've got in mind for him tonight, boss.' Jack smacked the lad's legs and said, 'Don't worry son – you're not playing.'

Jack has always enjoyed life and, as previously mentioned, his famous Scottish scouting trips were often spent on the banks of the Dee where the salmon leap far higher than Mick Harford.

Often the Chairman would ask, 'Where's the boss today, lads?' and Maurice or myself would pipe up, 'Looking at another player in Scotland, Mr Chairman.'

He must have wondered why we never signed a Scot!

Jack, though, is a marvellous man and I sampled his good-heartedness when I first went into television with *On the Ball* at London Weekend Television. Jack allowed me to do my show at lunchtime on Saturday and then join up with the team somewhere in the south if they were playing there, or to go on spying missions in the London area.

I always had a twinge of conscience about that though, and I once got the TV people to charter a helicopter to fly me up to Hillsborough for a big cup-tie with Arsenal. It was mid-winter and the pilot suggested we land at East Midlands Airport as the rotor blades were freezing up. At the airport I jumped into a taxi with a stunt driver type at the wheel, and we re-enacted a Hollywood car chase to get to the ground five minutes after kick-off. I arrived breathless in the dug-out and sat down next to Jack. He turned, looked at me quizzically, and said, 'What are you doing here?' The man was different class and, of course, still is.

Jack's hospitality at times ran to me staying with his family at their lovely home in the hills ... a courtesy he extended to his new signings too. I'll never forget one incident at the Charlton home. Jack's young lad Peter was messing around with a cane and despite repeated warnings from his Dad about being careful, he proceeded to knock over and break a valued ornament. Jack was after him in a flash and young Peter, knowing he was in trouble, ran for it, and in his haste slammed a door on his irate father's fingers.

There was blood everywhere and while Jack threatened all sorts against Peter, his wife wrapped a towel round the injury and I got the car ready for a hospital dash. When we arrived at the Outpatients at Barnsley Hospital, Jack's hand was in a right mess ... the towel practically holding two of his fingers together. We went up to reception, and the girl asked him his name and problem. 'It's my fingers ... they've been badly trapped. It's Charlton ... Jack Charlton.' The girl looked

up from her register in delighted surprise and, ignoring the blood-soaked towel, thrust her pen towards big Jack and said, 'Ooh Mr Charlton . . . can I have your autograph?'

Jack turned purple as he choked back the laughter. It was the only time I've ever heard him be rude to a lady. 'No,' or something to that effect, he answered in that colourful Geordie accent of his!

I'm told that the laughter has followed Jack and Maurice across the sea to Ireland . . . and I'm not surprised . . . they are one of the best double acts in the business, both on and off the field. I wish them well.

Football has always had its double acts. Every manager has his own coach and it is generally accepted that every boss will bring in his own man when taking over the reins at a new club. It's tough on the existing staff but it makes sense, for every boss needs his own trusted buffer between him and the players.

One double act I still keep in touch with through my coaching schools is the one which, north of the border, many Partick Thistle fans claim kept the popular Glasgow side in the Premier League during the late seventies – that of former Celtic hero Bertie Auld and my old Motherwell and Scotland team-mate, Pat Quinn.

Auld and Quinn were sheer showbusiness at Firhill. Bertie was the iron-hard manager who put the fear of death into players, demanding the same superb skills he showed himself as an inside-forward with the famous Lisbon Lions of Parkhead. Pat was the perfect foil, with his impish sense of humour and ability to put an arm around a chastised player and offer words of sympathy and advice.

The pair played the roles to perfection and of course the Thistle lads benefitted immensely, at times producing performances above and beyond the dreams of the Firhill faithful . . . like beating Rangers and Celtic there in the one season.

Bertie, who had learned under great coaches such as Jock Stein and Eddie Turnbull, was also fully aware of the value of press publicity. There was hardly a day when Bert, with his large cigar, was not featured in the Scottish press holding court about some issue or other . . . the net result putting an extra few thousand fans through the Firhill turnstiles.

Bertie and Pat, of course, did it all with a twinkle in their eyes, and even now they laugh at the day they fell out in spectacular fashion . . . and how Bertie's silver tongue got them out of hock with the press.

It happened during a relegation decider with Hearts. Defeat for either team would almost certainly mean relegation from the Premier League and a slump in gates in the First Division. The pressure was on and the Firhill dug-out was as frantic as ever, with Bertie blowing massive clouds of cigar smoke and giving everyone, including Pat, abuse.

Playing for Partick at the time was Jim Melrose, a fast young striker who, as Bertie says, 'would chase paper on a windy day'. Well, with Thistle leading 1–0 young Jim didn't chase after a ball Bertie felt he could have caught. 'Gerrimoff!' growled Bertie. 'Wasn't his ball,' shouted Pat. 'Gerrimoff I said!' howled Bertie, handing Pat the substitutes' board. 'Get stuffed!' replied Pat. 'Take him off yourself.' 'Your job,' shouted Bertie, as the subs' board flew from one end of the dug-out to the other. 'Don't be bloody daft!' shouted Pat. 'We've already used both subs!' Bertie, now uncontrollable, replied 'I don't care! GET HIM OFF! I WANT HIM OFF!'

Pat, mouthing curses, skulked to the touchline and held the board aloft to the roars of disbelief from the Thistle fans.

Thistle, left with ten men, amazingly scored another goal. Thistle won 2–0 and were safe. Hearts were doomed . . . and so it seemed was Bertie as the press waited at the end to hear the reason for the strangest managerial decision of the season. As the euphoria of the great escape took over, Bertie and Pat drew up the battle plans. 'You feed them drink,' said Bertie, 'I'll do the talking.'

It didn't take long before the question was posed 'Why take off Melrose and leave yourself with ten men when it was obvious he wasn't injured?' As Pat choked on his drink, Bertie drew long and hard on a new cigar and commented: 'Well lads, you might remember a month ago we were left with ten men in a match and we didn't handle the situation too well. Well today I felt we were so much on top that I could afford to see if the lads had learned anything in the last four weeks, so that if the ten-man situation ever came up again, we would cope with it.'

As the assembled press stood open-mouthed, Bertie flicked some ash from the end of the cigar and added, 'And of course they had . . . after all we went on to wrap it all up with that great goal. Have another drink, lads.'

A couple of real characters. Bertie has a wealth of stories and he told me one about my old boss Shanks I had never heard before. Apparently when Celtic became the first British team to win the European Cup by beating Inter Milan 2–1 in Lisbon in 1967, Shanks, a great admirer of the late Jock Stein, was on the Celtic team coach travelling back into town after the victory.

As the team rejoiced, Shankly thrust his hand into that of his great friend Stein and said, 'John – you're immortal.' And in football terms the old boy, as usual, was right.

Another manager in the same mould as Shankly and Stein and who, coincidentally, was a great friend of both was Don Revie, who tragically died of motor neurone disease this year. Don, like the other two, admired great talent, and while manager of Leeds United attempted to buy one of my all-time Scottish greats – Jim Baxter, then with Raith Rovers. The Don was known as a strict disciplinarian, so not surprisingly during the transfer negotiations asked my old Scotland team-mate

Don Revie who died tragically in 1989

about his personal life. 'I've heard a rumour that you smoke, drink, gamble and go out with women,' commented Don to Jim.

'You've got good information,' replied the bold one ... cocky even in those early days. Jim later joined Rangers!

One of Jim's big buddies at Sunderland was little George Mulhall, who also played for Scotland as a lively left-winger. George eventually became a manager himself – of Halifax Town – where he did what I would have thought was impossible: con my old boss Shanks.

Shanks was a sucker for big players. When he spotted big Alan Waddle playing for Halifax Town he was hooked, he wanted him for Anfield.

Now Alan was a big lad ... he wore size fourteen boots and the gag in football was that the old woman who lived in a shoe could have kept her entire family in his Hush Puppies. Anyway, George Mulhall could not believe his luck when Shanks phoned him at The Shay to inquire about big Alan. This was George's big chance to make some real money for the club ... but he had one problem: he hadn't a clue as to the whereabouts of his giant 'goldmine'. Eventually, George tracked down the big fellow to a fairground in Scarborough and he told him, 'Get ready for Liverpool, lad.'

To his amazement his star striker admitted two things:

1 He didn't know where Liverpool was!
2 He didn't have any shoes to wear.

It was here George revealed all the cunning which had made him a star winger with Aberdeen, Sunderland and Scotland. He wheeled big Alan into the nearest shoe shop and

George Mulhall, a lively left-winger who once conned Shanks

bought him the highest-heeled platform shoes anyone had seen pre-Elton John.

Hours later, Waddle was standing on the Anfield pitch, his head almost touching the crossbar when Shanks arrived to complete the transfer.

My old boss was overwhelmed at the size of his new white hope. 'Jesus Christ, the lad's a giant!' he gasped. 'I'll sign him.' Exit George, chuckling and grasping a large Liverpool cheque.

Mind you, George admits he never signed anyone at The Shay which is not, shall we say, the most picturesque of grounds. The little fellow used to meet potential new signings at a motorway service station miles away. 'I didn't want them to see what they were coming to,' he admits.

What chapter about managers would be complete without at least one story about the man himself . . . Cloughie.

Now Cloughie is in the mould of great managers such as Shankly, Stein and Revie. Like them, he is not backward at coming forward when it comes to putting players in their place. It's fair to say that one of Brian's most colourful signings at Forest was that of Justin Fashanu for one million pounds from Norwich City back in 1981. Justin was one of the snappiest dressers at the City Ground but unfortunately he didn't take his sartorial sharpness on to the field of play . . . after his successful spell at Norwich the goals dried up on him.

One day Justin was sauntering down the corridor from the dressing room when the manager stopped him in his tracks. Justin was wearing a bright green suit and a stetson. 'What on earth do you look like, young man?' rasped the unimpressed Mr Clough.

That big lad, Alan Waddle, here wearing size 14 boots whilst playing for Liverpool after his signing by Shanks

'I'm trying to be different,' retorted the indignant young trendsetter.

Cloughie as usual had an answer. 'If you want to be different, trying scoring a goal,' he raged. Justin left quietly.

It's well known in football that not all managers and players see eye to eye, and one of my favourite football stories concerns Tommy McAnearney, who was a wing-half for Sheffield Wednesday and later managed Aldershot.

One day while with the Shots, Tommy and his men faced up to a difficult away game at Hartlepool. All went well for forty-four minutes but then, on the stroke of half-time, their centre-half went up for a cross and the ball flew off the top of his head into his own net.

The disconsolate Aldershot players trooped off, expecting a real rollicking from Tommy in the dressing room. Amazingly though, McAnearney sat quiet in a corner for some time before speaking. But the words were well worth hearing. 'What time was that goal scored?' he asked. 'The forty-fourth minute boss,' piped up defender Joe Jopling.

'Brilliant!' shouted McAnearney. 'I've won the golden goal competition,' waving his winning ticket at a disbelieving team.

The same character is the subject of one of the daftest football quiz questions. What team had three managers at the same time? Answer: Aldershot ... Tommy, Mac and Ernie!

Get it?

Another Tommy who made a bit of a name for himself as a manager in his time is one of my favourite football characters, Tommy Docherty. Tom, as skipper of Scotland, took me under his wing in my early international days and we have been firm friends ever since ... and his stories always make me laugh.

The Doc, who claims to have had more clubs than Jack Nicklaus and been in more courts than Bjorn Borg, is as sharp as a tack and has that wonderful knack of laughing at himself as well as the world in general.

One of the best from him was when he was going through his infamous court case. He stepped into a hotel lift and the attendant turned to him and inquired, 'Going down, sir?' To which Tommy quipped: 'I certainly hope not.'

During his stint as manager of Manchester United, Tommy took United to Wembley in successive seasons, 1976 and 1977.

On the first of those visits he called in at the hotel's barber shop for a shave before the match. His quick shave and brush up cost him fifty pence. United duly lost the final to Southampton and the Doc returned to the hotel on the Monday for another tidy up. This time though he was charged three quid. 'How come?' asked the Doc. 'After all, it was only fifty pence on Saturday.'

The barber, sharper than his razor, replied, 'Well sir, your face is longer today, isn't it?'

Doc laughed, as he would. Now he's trying to make a living out of a one-man show touring the halls. I wish him well ... he's a very funny man.

Bill McGarry was known as a hard manager and when he arrived at Molineux as boss of Wolves, he knew he had a handful in a player known throughout the country as 'The Doog', alias of course Derek Dougan.

Now big Derek was never known to shun publicity. Who will ever forget the mohawk style haircut he sported during the early seventies? The Doog , like Tommy Doc, had an answer for everything. McGarry, in his introductory team talk to Derek and others, said, 'I don't want you to like me.'

Tommy Docherty, who claims to have had more clubs than Jack Nicklaus, seen here at Altrincham

'The Doog' has an answer for everything

Managing a football club can be a precarious business, and too much like a tightrope walk for my taste. Dear old Joe Mercer, a master manager in his days at Sheffield United, Aston Villa and Manchester City, gave this summary of the job: 'To manage a football club you need the skin of a rhinoceros, the luck of a pools winner and, above all, a good sense of humour so that you can laugh during the bad times as well as the good.'

To prove that managers do have senses of humour I have collected the following stories from my pals in the game, just for a laugh . . .

Tommy Docherty, the king of the one-liners, said of one of his full-backs when manager of Chelsea: 'I've seen milk turn faster.'

When the Doc was shortlisted for the Chelsea job he told the directors: 'If you appoint one of the others you won't get a coach. You'll get a hearse.' They fell about laughing and gave him the job.

One day during his spell as Manchester United boss, the Doc walked into the medical room to find striker Stuart Pearson lying on the treatment table.

'What's wrong with you?' he asked.

'I've got a bad back,' said Pearson.

'Don't worry, son,' said the Doc. 'Manchester City have got two.'

The Doc was once asked while he was manager of United if he had ever received any death threats. 'Only one,' said Docherty, with a deadpan face. 'A supporter wrote to me and threatened that if I picked a certain goalkeeper again he'd kill himself!'

Malcolm Macdonald recalls that when he was manager of Fulham he organised a Friday morning training session, and watched from the sidelines as his coach put the players through a sequence of exercises.

'When it was over,' says Malcolm, 'I called our skipper Les Strong over and said to him in front of the rest of the squad, "Les, I have to tell you that you have just completed the

Something I feel he might have regretted several years later when, after a series of rows between the two men, the Doog reminded him: 'I'm merely carrying out your instructions!'

Greavsie

I was once asked by a League club chairman if I would be interested in managing his club. 'You MUST be joking,' I said. 'I like my sanity too much to even consider it.'

84

Above: Malcolm Macdonald grabbing his fourth of five goals for England against Cyprus, 1975

Right: Rodney Marsh – 'famous for his cutting tongue as well as his stunning skill'

worst training session I have ever seen in all my years in the game as a player and as a manager." He let this pretty strong stuff sink in and then replied, "Oh come on, boss, I've been far worse than that!" '

Rodney Marsh was famous for his cutting tongue as well as his stunning skill. When Gordon Jago was introduced to the players as the new manager of Queen's Park Rangers, Rodney welcomed him with the words: 'The best of luck, boss. You will find us all behind you fifty per cent.'

The flamboyant Marsh, who has become a successful coach and manager in the United States, tells the story of how Fulham manager Vic Buckingham took him out on a deserted pitch at Fulham early in his career and told him, 'Now listen very carefully, son, I want you to learn from this . . .'

Buckingham then proceeded to do a soft-shoe shuffle as he sang the song 'I've Got Rhythm.'

Marsh looked on open-mouthed. When he had finished singing Buckingham said, 'That's all there is to it. Don't forget. It's called rhythm.'

Buckingham, an elegant and sometimes eccentric character, once called a players' meeting at Fulham that mystified everybody. Allan Clarke, then a young Fulham player who has since become a respected manager, recalls: 'It was a Friday. We all congregated in the dressing room at Craven Cottage and waited for what we thought would be a tactical talk about the next day's match.

'Vic came in and totally ignored every one of us. He picked up a newspaper, read the sports pages and then walked out of the dressing room without saying a word. We didn't see him for the rest of the day.

'The stunned silence he left behind him was finally broken by our goalkeeper Tony Macedo, who started singing, "Good morning . . . good morning . . ." '

Ted Drake, my first manager in football when I first started out with Chelsea, passes on a gem of a story from his playing days when he was England's barnstorming centre-forward. He takes us back into another world that is a million miles away from today's golden contracts and negotiating agents:

'I was playing for Southampton when footballers were on a maximum wage of eight pounds in the winter and six pounds in the summer. George Kay, the man who captained West Ham in the first ever FA Cup Final at Wembley was our manager. Before each season started you used to have to queue up to negotiate your terms for the following year.

'Remember that clubs could pay you less than the maximum, so you can imagine how anxious we used to get as we waited to agree our wages with the manager. On this particular day our full-back Albert Roberts was first in to see the manager. We crowded around him when he came out of the office and asked him what he'd got. Albert, a Yorkie from Goldthorpe, said, "Seven pounds ten in the season and a fiver in the summer. I'm reet disappointed, but there's nowt I can do about it."

'I was next in and was ready for a verbal battle to try to get the maximum. But I didn't have to say much. "Well, young Ted, you've had a great season," the manager said. "There are clubs interested in you, but we've decided we're not letting you go. You'll be pleased to know that we're going to pay you the maximum eight pounds in the season and six in the summer."

' "Thank you, Mr Kay," I said politely and then went out and reported to my team-mates. Our wing-half Stan Woodhouse was the next man in. "You had a good season and we're very pleased with you," George Kay told him. "We will pay you eight pounds in the winter and five pounds in the summer."

'Stan, a Warrington lad, said, "Ee, but Mr Kay, you've just given young Ted eight and six."

' "Aye, 'appen I have," said Mr Kay, who was also a Lancastrian. "But he's a better player than you."

'Stan pondered on this for a moment and then came back with a blinder: "But he's not a better player than me in the summer." '

Harry Storer was one of the great character-managers in the immediate post-war years and was Brian Clough's inspiration when he first came into management. Joe Mercer tells this Storer story . . .

Ted Drake – paid eight pounds in winter and six
pounds in summer

'It was in my early days as manager at Sheffield United. We'd played Harry's Derby County side and they had put the boot about a bit. When I saw Harry after the match I said: "I don't know why you bothered to put the ball on the pitch. Two of your players didn't need one. They kicked us instead."

' "Oh," said Harry, "which two are you referring to? I want their names."

'Well I didn't want to get anybody into trouble, but Harry insisted on me naming them.

Peter Shreeves

' "I'll tell you who they are provided you don't punish them," I said.

' "Punish them?" said Harry loudly. "I'm not going to take any action against them. It's the other nine I'm after!" '

My favourite Harry Storer tale concerns a Derby County forward who was summoned to see Harry one Monday morning following a defeat on the Saturday. He took the player out on to the pitch and got on to his all fours in front of one of the goals and started searching around as if he had lost something.

' "What are you looking for, boss?" asked the startled player.

' "The bloody hole you were hiding in on Saturday," yelled Storer.'

Managers have got to learn to laugh with their players if they're going to win their respect. Peter Shreeves spins this yarn from his days as assistant manager to Keith Burkinshaw at Tottenham: 'We were on a club tour of Japan, and we were scheduled to pay an official visit to the British Embassy in Tokyo. Terry Naylor, one of the club jokers, convinced Keith that it was the custom for visitors to the Embassy to remove their shoes and socks before entering the main reception room.

'Once he had got Keith hooked, Terry primed the rest of us and when we got to the Embassy we all went through the motions of untying our shoelaces. Then Keith led us all into the guest room to meet the ambassador and, of course, our manager was the only barefooted person in the building.'

Terry Neill, former Arsenal and Tottenham manager, swears the following story is true and no Irish blarney:

'A team preparing to go out to play a vital relegation battle had their usual encouragement, stimulation and motivation from the manager and coach in the dressing room prior to the game. In fact, the players were at such a pitch they could easily have torn the walls down. Then, just as they were about to leave the dressing room, the manager barred their way at the door for what they thought was going to be one last rallying call. "Just one more thing, you lot," he said with true feeling in his voice. "What ever you do – don't let them panic you into playing football." '

Terry Neill was always trying to think of novel ideas to enliven pre-match tactical talks, as this Arsenal story from Alan Ball illustrates: 'We were on a close-season tour of Switzerland, and before one of the games Terry came into the dressing room carrying a brown paper bag. We watched wide-eyed as he took out eleven toy cowboys. They were all shooting pistols and rifles. He set them out in team formation, and then from the bag he took out another handful of toys. These were Red Indians. After setting them out on the opposite side of the make-believe pitch he swept the Indians on to the floor with the palm of his hand. "That's what I want you to do to the opposition," he said. "Go out and destroy them . . . just like that!" '

Malcolm Allison has been one of my favourite people in football. He can be outrageous at times, but the game is richer for his personality, and there are few who match

his flair and tactical understanding. Big Mal tells this lovely story of when he was manager at Crystal Palace with Terry Venables as his right-hand man:

'Terry and I went to Darlington to watch their League match against Doncaster with a view to buying a player. The Darlington directors gave us the full VIP treatment. There we were, two flash Londoners playing the big "I am" and the Darlington people couldn't do enough for us because they thought we might be spending some money on one of their players.

'When it was time for the kick-off we were shown to the best seats in the house, right in the front row of the directors' box. We sat on converted cinema seats that had been bought from a bankrupt picture palace. Many people in the crowd, curious as to what we were doing in Darlington, kept looking at us more than at the game.

'Suddenly there was a loud cracking noise and our seats collapsed under us. Terry and I were left sitting on the ground looking over the top of the directors' box like a couple of Chad characters.

Malcolm Allison – one of Greavsie's favourite people in football

90

'Everybody roared with laughter to see the two "flash Harrys" brought down to earth with a bump. Terry and I looked at each other with one of those "that's another fine mess you've got me into, Stanley" stares, and then self-consciously picked ourselves up and moved to seats at the back of the box. After that we always claimed we brought the house down at Darlington!'

Have you heard the one about the Irishman who was sacked as manager of a First Division club while sitting in the back of a London taxi? Johnny Carey, then in charge of fifth-placed Everton, was sharing a cab ride with his chairman John Moores after a Football League meeting in London in 1961. Moores, who was Littlewoods chairman, gave Carey the shock news of his dismissal as the taxi crawled through rush-hour traffic.

'I let Mr Moores pay the fare,' said Carey with his typical Irish wit. 'I knew in my own mind that I was not a failure and that's all that mattered to me. I have since been very wary about sharing a cab with anybody!'

Billy Bingham was another Irish manager of Everton. When he introduced his new sign-

Billy Bingham predicted his own sacking!

ing Duncan McKenzie to the press, he said with a laugh, 'The last time a manager signed him, he got the sack a couple of weeks later! He could become very unpopular with managers.' Sure enough, a few weeks later Billy got the sack – just as Brian Clough had done shortly after buying McKenzie for Leeds.

Duncan is also one of the central characters in a story that has been relayed to me about that most Yorkshire of Yorkshiremen Danny Williams, who was manager of Mansfield when Duncan arrived on loan from Nottingham Forest.

Danny organised a training match to get Duncan used to playing the Mansfield way. The pitch was six inches deep in mud and Danny stood on the touchline wearing galoshes and with his trouser-bottoms tucked into his socks. Danny, who had played more than five hundred matches for Rotherham after joining them from a colliery team, talked with a Yorkshire accent that makes Freddie Trueman and Harvey Smith sound like posh southerners. Well, almost!

'Thee lad,' he called from the touchline, referring to Duncan. 'I want thee to play out wide on t'left.'

Duncan did what he was told and got nowhere.

Danny stopped the game. 'Aw reet then. Now I want thee to play out on t'right.'

Again, McKenzie could not get into the game. Danny scratched his head, and then tried again. 'Reet, now this time I want thee to go in't middle and play alongside Wiggy [former England centre-forward Frank Wignall] and feed off t'big feller.'

But McKenzie could still not make any impact. Right, left, centre . . . Danny had tried all the permutations. He was wondering what to do next when a Mansfield player who knew McKenzie well sidled up and said quietly, 'Boss, why not just let him do his own thing?'

Danny clapped his hands together to inspire some enthusiasm. 'Reet, Duncan, go where you bloody like,' he said. Within a minute of the restart McKenzie dummied past two defenders, dribbled round another and then chipped the ball over the oncoming goalkeeper and into the net.

Danny blew his whistle. 'Reet then, lads – that'll do for me. T'training's o'er wi' for today.'

Stan Cullis, the manager who worked wonders with Wolves in the fifties, was tearing off his players following a poor performance when he noticed out of the corner of his eye that one of the reserves was giggling. 'I don't know what you've got to laugh at,' roared Cullis. 'You're not even good enough to get into the team!'

Ron Atkinson is one of the wittiest managers in the game. When he was manager of West Bromwich Albion, Atko was friendly with the then Birmingham City boss Jim 'Bald Eagle' Smith. One evening they went together to see comedian Billy Connolly, who was appearing in Brum.

After the show they were invited into the Big Yin's dressing room. Smithy asked Billy if he found it easy to communicate with Midland audiences.

'Och aye,' said Billy. 'I enjoy playing Birmingham.'

'Don't we all,' said Atko. 'Don't we all.'

In his first season at Old Trafford, Lancashire Cricket Club borrowed the ground for a floodlit cricket match. As the groundsmen were marking out the 22-yard cricket strip in the middle of the pitch Atko suddenly summoned Ray Wilkins to join him on the touchline. 'Look, Ray,' he said, pointing at the cricket strip. 'They've marked out your territory.'

Ray used to take terrible stick from Atkinson, who used to call him 'The Crab' because he reckoned he only moved sideways. Tommy Docherty once said of Ray when he was skip-

Stan Cullis, manager who worked wonders for
Wolves in the fifties

pering United: 'The only time he goes forwards is for the toss-up before the kick-off.'

I have been delighted to see Ray silencing all his critics with a procession of positive performances for Rangers. It was at Ibrox where Scot Symon, Rangers' manager for nine successful years from 1956, was infamous for his insistence on not talking to the press.

A journalist once telephoned him at Ibrox on the day of a scheduled midweek match. 'If this fog doesn't lift there isn't much chance of the match being played tonight, is there?' said the reporter in a conversational tone.

'I never comment on the weather,' snapped Symon, and put the phone down.

Gordon Milne, former Leicester City and Coventry manager and my old England teammate who used to play with Saint at Liverpool, passes on this true story about a player who must remain anonymous:

'The club trainer was getting sick to death with having his medical supplies and stock of chewing gum raided by an unknown player. It went on for weeks until the trainer could stand it no longer. He decided he would catch the culprit. He replaced the chewing gum in his locker with an identical-looking brand of laxatives.

'The raids continued unabated until one morning the trainer received a telephone call from the wife of one of the first-team players. "He won't be in for training today," she said. "God knows what's upset him, but he's hardly been out of the toilet all night."

'The trainer put the telephone down with a smile of satisfaction on his face.'

Stan Mortensen, the former Blackpool bomber who scored Wembley's only FA Cup Final hat-trick in the 1953 victory over Bolton, tells this tale about former Blackpool manager Joe Smith: 'We were playing in Cardiff late one season. It was a desperate match for us. Defeat would have meant relegation to the Second Division.

'Just before we were due to go out on to the pitch, Joe Smith walked in looking in deadly earnest. "I want everybody out of this dressing room except the eleven players," he announced.

'The trainers, the reserves and a couple of hangers-on all trooped out. We all looked at each other and wondered what was coming. "Surely he's not going to give us a tactics talk, skip." I said to our captain Harry Johnston. "Well, it'll be the first one he's ever given if he does," said Harry.

'Joe was one of those managers who believed in letting his team play it off the cuff, and he considered tactical talks a waste of breath. He waited until just the players were in earshot. Then he said in a confidential tone and with a Churchillian delivery, "I can't express how important it is that as soon as the game's over you are in and out of the bath as quickly as possible. We don't want to miss the 5.15 train back to Blackpool."

'At this Joe walked out of the dressing room leaving us looking at each other in amazement. By the way, we won the match 3–0 *and* caught the train.'

8 SUFFOLK PUNCHLINES

Ipswich is sometimes wrongly cast as one of the soccer outposts of English football. In this chapter, Greavsie rights that wrong with some humorous stories from Portman Road, reflecting the skills and humour of some of the men who have pushed the club to the forefront of British football.

As an Essex man, I look on the football folk of Ipswich as near neighbours – and have always done so. The club has given me huge enjoyment in football over the years I've been involved in the game.

While I was playing non-league football with Barnet, the first result I looked for in the newspapers was that of Ipswich, under my old mate Bobby Robson. Robbo did a wonderful job for Ipswich – leading them to European honours – and only bad luck prevented them winning the First Division title itself.

It was a sign of Bobby Robson's expertise that a little club like Ipswich should gain such stature in the game, not only in Britain, but in Europe – and as far as I am concerned, nothing has changed during his days as England manager.

Getting serious, I believe some of the popular press have been disgraceful in their castigation of Robson. The man has led England to World Cups and European Championships and has a record which stands alongside some of the great bosses – but because some jumped-up sports editor who's never played the game and known the pressures of management decides that he's a failure, then he and his family suffer appallingly.

Bobby Robson did a 'wonderful job for Ipswich'

Enough said about that. Let's dwell on the great and funny days of Ipswich – days which put the club on the map. East Anglia is something of a backwater, most people feel. It is only a freak of geography, they say, that most of it isn't in the North Sea. Have you ever tried to drive to Portman Road? You can get to Paris quicker. They are one hundred miles from the nearest First Division club . . . so no wonder they make a fuss of a local derby at Norwich 45 miles away. It's only a stone's throw!

Most professional footballers who've played for either Norwich or Ipswich grow to like the area. You stumble into a surprising number who return after their playing days. It's a good life in that part of the world . . . and they can usually look back on a few laughs. Things haven't changed much, although it is some time since any Norwich players have been brought to court for poaching!

It happened in Lol Morgan's time. Do you remember names like Bill Punton, Barry Butler, and of course Ron Davies? In Bill's time – he still lives and works in Norwich and manages a local team – the lads had a taste for country pursuits. The local constabulary knew that perhaps not everything was quite within the law . . . and they kept a close eye on their post-match activities.

But the boys, led by one Taffy Williams, were sharp. They did their poaching from a car – on the move. Shoot, hit the target, grab it – and go. Except, they were caught when, in the excitement of the chase, one of them forgot to wind the window down . . . and found that the damage to the car, the shotguns and the bootful of pheasants were difficult to explain at the police roadblock round the corner.

It didn't do their standing any harm in Nor-

Allan Hunter probably doesn't want to be reminded of that little accident!

96

wich apparently. When their case was heard, the magistrate said half the local population wouldn't understand the charge; the other half would wonder what all the fuss was about.

The area isn't as quiet as it looks – and the football clubs always turn out some unlikely tales. We don't need to go into detail about why Bobby Robson wouldn't answer phone calls in the early days – when he was pursued by a player's wife . . . to abuse him, as it happened, because he had dropped her husband.

There have always been characters at the club, encouraged in many ways by the style of management. Allan Hunter was a battling Irishman who played for Ipswich for many years. If you bump into him, don't remind him of the day he missed an important Championship game because he tripped over his dog's lead when he took it for a walk at night. He took a lot of stick over that. But Clive Woods still laughs about the day he was ruled out for a few games – he damaged his back trying to swat a wasp with a rake when he was doing

some gardening. Now when did that ever happen to a Chelsea or Arsenal player?

Ipswich Town is the club where they always used to say: 'The only crisis is when we run out of dry white wine in the boardroom.'

Former Chairman, the late John Cobbold, created the easy-going atmosphere at a club where two England managers, Sir Alf Ramsey and Bobby Robson, made their names. Where else would a Chairman let a new manager get away with what Bill McGarry (a Portman Road Second Division-winning boss in 1968) said to 'Mr John' on the day he arrived?

The jovial Town Chairman was introducing McGarry to the playing staff in the dressing room after his move from Bournemouth. After the hellos were over, McGarry turned to his new Chairman and said, 'That's the last time you'll be coming in my bloody dressing room.'

McGarry was a hard man and his successor, Robson, needed to be when the fists began flying soon after his arrival to take charge in 1969, not long after his sacking at Fulham. Senior players resented the new young boss who was not much older than themselves and old hands Billy Baxter and Tommy Carroll were involved in the corridor fracas with him.

After two years struggling near the foot of the First Division table Robson feared the sack after the crowd had chanted for his head during a 3–1 home defeat by Manchester United on a night when George Best ran riot for the Reds.

An emergency board meeting was called the following morning and the current England chief went in to it, fearing the worst. To his surprise, a smiling 'Mr John' apologised for the crowd's behaviour and cracked open a bottle of champagne. 'Mr John' used to say: 'At Ipswich if we win we have a bottle of champagne, if we lose we have two.'

Fellow Chairmen and Directors who took the game too seriously did not interest 'Mr John' and there was a good example after one particular match when he walked into the inner boardroom to confront the Chairman of a northern club. 'Would you like a drink?' asked 'Mr John'. 'Nay lad, no alcohol has ever passed my lips,' came the reply from the Chairman who was also a council alderman and former mayor.

'Cigar perhaps?' was the next invitation extended.

'Nay lad, never smoked in me life.'

With this the Ipswich Chairman retorted: 'In that case I don't think you and I have a great deal in common.'

The late Lady Blanche Cobbold, mother to John and brother Patrick, the currect Chairman, was a very quick-witted person also and one of her classics came at Wembley in 1978 when Robson's team were beating Arsenal to lift the FA Cup for the only time in their history. Asked if she would like to meet the Prime Minister, she said: 'I'd rather have a gin and tonic.'

Former chief scout Ron Gray was a great character of the club who had a trick up his sleeve when English Schools' FA officials banned scouts from watching a North versus South trial at Loughborough.

Determined not to miss out, Ron paid a school caretaker some cash for the loan of his overalls, wheelbarrow and broom. He then walked in and watched from the touchline – later signing two players for the club.

During the early Robson days of struggle at Portman Road, before the club began to soar, scout Gray went to the 'gaffer's' office to give a report on a player he watched up in the far north the previous night.

ROBSON: 'Is he strong, Ron?'
GRAY: 'Built like an ox, boss.'

Sir Alf Ramsey – another England manager who made his name at Ipswich

ROBSON: 'Is he good in the air, Ron?'

GRAY: 'Heads it like a rocket, boss.'

ROBSON: 'Has he got two good feet, Ron?'

GRAY: 'Certainly has, boss.'

By this time Robson, desperate for a new striker, is getting very excited.

ROBSON: 'Shall we sign him then, Ron?'

GRAY: 'No, boss.'

ROBSON: 'Why not?'

GRAY: *'Because he can't play!'*

The Ipswich Town youth policy was the secret of their glory days success when for many years they challenged constantly at the top of the First Division table and were regularly in Europe, winning the UEFA Cup in 1981. The 1975 FA Youth Cup Final saw them beat West Ham at Portman Road in a second leg watched by a crowd of 16,000.

After that match all the parents of the team were treated to a banquet at a plush hotel and the best rooms were reserved for them to stay the night. On that evening the last word went to who else but Chairman 'Mr John', who said: 'We have all enjoyed a great night and I hope you parents have had a good time. Now I want you all to go to your rooms and produce another cup-winning youth side for us in six-teen years' time!'

Another saying of his was: 'They say that at Ipswich it is all wine, women and song. This is not true – we don't do any singing!'

When Robson left, his successor Bobby Ferguson had a reputation for cracking the whip. But 'Fergy' also liked a laugh and a joke. He admits to once going into the oppo-sition dressing room at Manchester United by mistake and beginning his team talk.

This was back in 1984 with Old Trafford packed to see a game where United needed to stay in the title hunt, and Town had to gain victory if they were to avoid the drop to the Second Division. He left the referee's room with a copy of the United side half an hour before kick-off and walked down the corridor,

looking over the names on the official team list. Then he barged open a dressing-room door and, with head down, caught a glimpse of a dark-skinned player he thought was his Dutch midfield man Romeo Zondervan.

It was, in fact, United's Remi Moses and Bobby was in the United dressing room having begun his team talk!

Mich D'Avray, scorer of one of the goals in the match that Ipswich won 2–1, recalls: 'There was a lot of tension in our young team. Bobby's bloomer, which he freely admitted, gave us all a lift and a good laugh to help us feel a bit better. I am convinced it helped us to win that day.'

Trevor Putney was always a great dress-ing-room character at Ipswich before his move up the road to East Anglian rivals Nor-wich. 'Putters' once went to watch a reserve match at Portman Road in which his close friend and business partner, Mark Grew, now with Port Vale, was playing in goal. He wandered into the Press Association box and when the announcer wasn't looking put his voice to the microphone. Grew picked up the ball and threw it out and the startled crowd heard the cockney tones of 'Well done "Bar-ney" [Grew's nickname]. See you tonight.'

Boss Ferguson was in the directors' box and recognised the voice immediately. He dashed to the dressing-room area to have a colourful exchange with 'Putters'.

Putney was later seen wandering around the club car park exclaiming: 'What's the matter with this club? There's no fun any more.'

Ferguson saw the funny side all right but

Opposite top: Mich d'Avray – a young player in a young Ipswich team

Opposite bottom: Trevor Putney – once tagged the 'Flying Maggot' by his manager

had to make a stand as he couldn't afford to have player power on the 'mike'.

Putney, once tagged the 'Flying Maggott' by Ferguson in training, got himself sent off the following season just before the end of a match at Newcastle. At that time Ipswich were ahead and the sending off disrupted things to such an extent that the game was lost.

Fearing the wrath of no-nonsense Geordie Ferguson, Putney disappeared for an hour after the game and hopped on the team bus at the last minute, knowing that his manager was staying in his native north east over the weekend.

Current Ipswich manager John Duncan comes out with some crackers from time to time and, when asked if he was sleeping all right at a time last season when the Second Division promotion push was at its height, he replied: 'I sleep like a baby. I wake up crying four times every night!'

Duncan is one of the renowned touchline remonstrators. Last season he was warned by the referee after a bout of coaching from the dug-out. But he pointed to coach Peter Trevivian and said: 'It was him.'

Poor Peter then got the rest of the dressing down from the referee.

Former Tottenham striker Duncan said to one of his players last season: 'You only played one bad ball all afternoon. It was that white one!'

Another great character who always gave me a laugh was Mike Channon who, to my mind, was one of the best England inside-forwards of recent years. Mike finally won a League Cup medal with Norwich City at Wembley in the twilight of his career – and during that time he often appeared on ITV's Big Match series.

But just as Saint described big Jack's lack of memory with players' names, so did I laugh at Mike's mispronunciations. During England's World Cup campaign of 1986, Mike went through a fortnight mispronouncing Gary Lineker's name. On the last day, determined to get it right, he turned to studio host Brian Moore, beamed proudly and described the English striker as 'GARY LINE-ACRE'. 'There, I got it right at last,' laughed Mike. 'No you didn't, old mate,' said Mooro. 'You got it absolutely wrong again!' The studio erupted and so did Mike.

The Carrow Road crowd loved his days with Norwich – but I have a feeling he signed for the Canaries just to be near Newmarket Races!

At Ipswich the rapport between directors and players has always been special. It was once typified by former Ipswich and Northern Ireland defender Allan Hunter. 'Big Al', as the crowd used to call him, once arrived at the customs' checkpoint with a group of directors after a Town win in Europe.

Hunter went to a customs official and said, pointing to a senior director: 'This man is way over the limit. And it's all in his stomach!'

The last Ipswich word should go to John Cobbold, the club Chairman who bred donkeys, and could not take life too seriously. One afternoon he went to an executive box to watch a reserve match and ordered sandwiches together with the odd bottle of wine.

At five past three he looked at his watch and wondered what was going on – no players on the pitch and no crowd. No wonder . . . the reserves were playing away!

Ipswich Town was his life and he once said: 'I wouldn't cross the road to watch a game of football. But I'd travel a thousand miles to watch Ipswich Town.'

9 A RUB OF THE GREEN

Jim Craig, TV broadcaster, a former international full-back with Scotland and member of the famous 'Lisbon Lions' Celtic team which brought the European Cup to Britain for the first time in 1967, remembers his early days in Glasgow and the magic moments which made Celtic a grand old team to play for.

It's an interesting place is Glasgow. A city whose population has four main topics of conversation: the weather (generally hellish); politics (mainly Labour, or further to the left); religion (choice of Catholic or Protestant in the old days, now backed up by Sikh, Hindu, Muslim, Shinto, Buddhist or just plain Atheist); and football, where you lean either towards Rangers or Celtic, apart from a faithful few thousand who failed their 11-plus and support Partick Thistle or Clyde.

It was an equally fascinating place to grow up in and try to make the grade in football. You learned the rules early. The wet weather made for heavy grounds, so long studs were in. If the four nails (remember this was in the fifties) which held the stud to the sole were showing, then even better. They gripped the ground more efficiently and also gave better contact with your immediate opponent, as it wasn't only football, it was a religious battle.

You see, in Glasgow, the children are sent to separate schools, dependent on their parents' religious beliefs, and football matches between these schools have a passion all their own. As well as the usual shouts during the game – like 'my ball', 'here' or 'pass!' – there are others, especially indigenous to Glasgow, like 'Papish swine' or 'Prod-die pig'. This also led to all kids being asked at varying times that most awkward of Glaswegian questions (awkward depending on where you were at the time): 'Are you a Billy?' (a supporter of King William of Orange, therefore of the Protestant persuasion) 'or a Tim?' (short for Tim Malloy, rhymes with Bhoy, the nickname of Celtic FC and therefore of the Catholic faith.

The proper answer to this question, or let's say the answer which got you into least trouble, was easier if you knew the religious leanings of the person doing the questioning. Thus you could say you were a Protestant to another Protestant, or admit you were a Catholic to another of the same. If you were not sure about the interrogator's stance, you could always say you did not like football or, to come out with an even bigger lie, say you supported Queen's Park.

This religious divide led to some interesting incidents. It was well known to us that Celtic would sign players of any background, whereas Rangers would only sign Protestants. When trials for district or international teams were held, the famous

Jim Craig – former Celtic and Scotland full-back

104

Rangers' scout Jimmy Smith would come along. The players from Protestant schools, under the pressure of his scrutiny, would play very badly, while the boys from Catholic schools played magnificently, quite secure in the knowledge that, even if they performed like a cross between those famous players of the time, Stanley Matthews and Pele, they would never be signed by Rangers. Mind you, with Rangers' signing of Mo Johnston, times it would seem have changed!

The rivalry even got into church. A priest friend of mine told me that shortly after he was ordained he was giving a sermon on joy in all its forms and mentioned how natural it was that a successful result for your favourite team should provide such pleasure. He mentioned some scores: Rangers 2, Dundee 2; Hibernian 4, Celtic 5 etc. Just after Mass, he was standing outside the church meeting his flock, when an old man walked past, supporting himself with a stick. 'I enjoyed your sermon very much, Father,' he murmured, as he shuffled past. He then turned back towards the priest, '. . . but did you have to give the Rangers a draw?!'

My own professional career began when I was signed by manager Jimmy McGrory for Celtic in January 1965. I was then taken into the club boardroom to meet the directors. I first met Chairman Robert Kelly who, as he had had a withered right arm since birth, held out his left hand to me, confusing me completely as to which hand I should use. I then met Secretary Desmond White, who had been struck on the right shoulder by a propeller during the war, and he also held out his left hand, putting me back into a position of utter discomfort as to my move. By the time I was brought face-to-face with the third Celtic director, I was totally at sea, quite convinced that this was club custom. Fortunately, this director, Tom Devlin, saw the puzzled look on my face, burst out laughing, gave me a usual right hand to shake and explained the above details.

As I had gone from school to university football, where training was fairly interesting with a lot of emphasis on ballwork, I was really looking forward to the professional game. I'm afraid, at first, I was not impressed. Training consisted of lapping the track, 440s, 220s, straights, 50-yard sprints etc. The theory behind it was that if you were deprived of the ball in midweek, you would be all the more eager for it on Saturday. It was a bit like training for snooker by mountain climbing. In fact, when you ran down the tunnel on a Saturday afternoon, we had to make a conscious effort to run on to the pitch. Our impulse as we reached the running track was to turn right and keep going!

Then there was the kit for training. Short-sleeve shirt, jockstrap and shorts, with heavy jersey over the top. That jersey was double thickness, crew-necked and provided at pre-season training every year. For the first few months, we spent every spare moment at training pulling the top away from our necks so that it was easier to breathe. By the time we had made it into a V-necked outfit, winter had arrived and we spent the next few months trying to pull it back up again!

Jock Stein once said (I think in a moment of weakness) that he was always open to suggestions regarding our playing or training conditions. I took him at his word and mentioned that it might be better if we received the heavy jersey at the beginning of winter. 'I'll keep it in mind,' was his cryptic reply, but when I came in to training the next day, my jersey had mysteriously disappeared and for two or three days I trained in a short-sleeved jersey – in November!

I must point out that the training schedule mentioned above was strictly in the pre-Stein

Jock Stein – always open to suggestions!

106

era. The Big Man revolutionised Celtic when he joined them and soon made his mark on the players.

I can recall with perfect clarity the sarcasm in his voice during training. To a new young player reluctant to shoot from a difficult angle – 'Take your time son, the television cameras are on their way'; to his pet hate, a goalkeeper going through a bad time – 'The way that ball keeps bouncing out of your hands, I think we'll call you Iron Gloves . . .' or 'Well, they've started heart transplants – they'll get round to hands soon . . .'; and to players training before an important game and not bothered about tackling too much – 'What do you think this is, a Mutual Admiration Society?!'

On one special occasion before an Old Firm game (Celtic *v* Rangers for the uninitiated) Sir Robert Kelly, Chairman of the club, came into the dressing room and warned the players about getting into trouble with the referee, about how much damage tough play did to the image of the club, and how the good of the game transcends every result. Jock Stein heard this out in silence, ushered Sir Robert out of the dressing room, shut the door and stood with his back to it. His first words left us in no doubt as to his feelings: 'Well, you can forget all that bloody nonsense for a start!'

Mind you, the Boss did not have an easy time of it in those days as he was surrounded by players whose little foibles could lead to various contretemps. Like Jimmy Johnstone, for instance, the only player I can ever recall leaving the field at full speed without the referee's permission (this was in Vienna, in a public park for a pre-season friendly). He sped past the bench and through adjacent pitches with us all looking after him in bemused fashion. We discovered later that he had had a sudden attack of diarrhoea.

The same Jimmy was substituted in a game against Dundee United by Jock Stein and on the way up the tunnel, shouted at the manager and threw his jersey at him. The Big Man lumbered up the tunnel after him, presumably to remonstrate with Jimmy. As I was leaving the ground later, a newspaper reporter (a newsman, as opposed to a sports reporter – a breed Jock did not like) asked: 'What are you going to do about the Johnstone incident?' Jock's reply was succinct. 'F*** off!' This was reported the next day as, 'When asked about the Johnstone incident, Mr Stein replied: "We will deal with the matter internally" . . .'

Tommy Gemmell also had his moments. I once had a night out in Malta with Tam when he introduced me to his favourite tipple – vodka and crème de menthe! I felt rough for about a fortnight!

Other memories of my team-mates come flooding back. Ronnie Simpson, who loved telling jokes, the cornier the better . . . 'Did you hear about the Irishman who couldn't understand why he had only two brothers and his sister had three?'

Ronnie was a most experienced goalkeeper, with two FA Cup winners' medals with Newcastle United in his possession, and was always worth listening to in the dressing room. He might have shouted good advice on the pitch as well, but unfortunately, he played without his dentures, and although he flapped his arms around and plenty of sounds came out of his mouth, I could never understand a word!

Bobby Murdoch was the most talented all-rounder of all. When he played, the team played. Unfortunately, he was beset by weight problems in the late sixties and struggled to maintain his form. Several visits to health farms slowly improved his condition.

In Bermuda in 1970, I was standing at the side of a superb training pitch in Hamilton, resting a groin strain and watching the boys training, when I was joined by an expatriate

Above: Tommy Gemmell's favourite tipple – vodka and crème de menthe

Right: Bobby Murdoch . . . 'most talented all-rounder of all'

Scot from Motherwell. He enthused at great length over the team's performance the Sunday before and how well the lads had played, 'especially Bobby Murdoch', he pointed as the player ran towards him to complete the penultimate leg of a sprint exercise. 'He looks in really good condition these days.' As if on cue, Bobby, who had been at a Caledonian Society reception the night before with the rest of us, stopped dead in his tracks, bent over and, with a violent heave, deposited his breakfast plus previous evening's meal all over the hallowed turf! At least that stopped my Motherwell friend from prattling on!

Billy McNeill and Chairman Sir Bob Kelly were both Lanarkshire men and had a very good relationship. When Celtic played Benfica in the European Cup in Lisbon in 1969, they played very badly to lose a three-goal lead from the Glasgow tie and eventually went through on the toss of a coin, the method used to decide a tie before penalty shoot-outs were introduced.

Naturally enough, everyone was delighted at our narrow escape and parties erupted in several rooms in the early hours. It was still a fairly exuberant group of players and officials who boarded the bus for the airport the next morning and as Billy McNeill got on, beaming from ear to ear, he said in a loud and cheerful voice to the Chairman, 'I hope we didn't disturb you with the noise we were making last night, Sir Robert?' The Chairman's first few words were a model of courtesy and gentleness. 'You didn't disturb me at all, Billy,'... but then the steel and loudness entered the voice for the classic put-down, 'but I don't know why you were celebrating anyway!'

John Clark was a quiet, very effective sweeper who was really bothered by prematch nerves and spent most of the time before the game locked in the toilet. His ritual was to come out of the WC, wash his hands –

and then go back in again!

Bertie Auld, on the other hand, looked completely at ease before a game, wise-cracking to all and sundry. 'I like the tin flute [suit], son,' he would say to a new young player. 'Thanks, Bert,' came the reply from the wearer, flattered by the attention. Then Bertie would come back on the attack. 'Aye, I remember my father used to wear clothes like that!' He would then turn round and pick another target, like the retreating back of John Clark. 'Hey, Luggy!' (Clark's nickname, so chosen because he once played a few games with a huge bandage covering an ear problem.) 'The club says the reason we're not getting bigger bonuses is that they're spending too much on toilet paper for you!' Too late, Luggy was in his pre-match hideaway and the door bolt was slammed home.

When the final whistle went in Lisbon, I made a bee-line for my team-mates to celebrate, but Bobby Lennox ran towards, then past me, on the halfway line and raced towards the Celtic goal before being swallowed up in the crowd. It was some hours later before I found out the reason. He had left his false teeth in Ronnie Simpson's cap at the back of the net so that he could slip them in before the Cup was presented. Apparently, he got to them just before the Celtic support who, on that day, would have taken ANY type of souvenir of the occasion.

Steve Chalmers could never be accused of making a quick decision. He was a great Volkswagen fan but in 1968, in St Etienne, he bought a car magazine about the new Renault 16 and, on the plane back, badgered me to use my very limited French to translate all the details. Almost every day for the next month, that bloody magazine was brought into training for me to decipher another bit, but by the end of that time, he said he had finally made up his mind that this was the car for him. Two days later, he turned up in a light-blue,

chrome-gleaming, aerial-sporting, truly immaculate – Volkswagen!

On that tour to Bermuda which I mentioned before, McNeill, Willie Wallace, Harry Hood and myself were looking over the stern of a large fishing launch while the then Chairman, Desmond White, strapped into his seat, wrestled with his catch. At last we spotted, way down in the blue water, a flash of silver. 'There it is, what is it?' we cried. The skipper of the craft replied in nonchalant fashion, 'A shark, about six or seven feet.' Well, those were the magic words for we four heroes who immediately retired to the upper deck, where we watched with interest as Mr White pulled his catch in and asked loudly, on more than one occasion, 'Are you sure this is safe?'

Bobby Lennox glides past Old Firm rivals, Colin Jackson and John Greig in the Scottish FA Cup Final, 1971

Finally, back to the man himself, Jock Stein, who always had his finger on the pulse and never seemed to sleep. He had a wee turn of phrase, too. In the European Cup Final of 1970, Celtic were not doing well in the second half against Feyenoord and the backroom staff were very well aware of that. 'We're really struggling,' said trainer Neilly Mochan, 'we'll need to put on a substitute.'

'You're right, Neilly,' replied Jock, and glanced to his right, where the subs, John Fallon, Tommy Callaghan, Harry Hood, George Connelly and myself, immediately started to tighten laces and pull up socks. However, our hopes were soon dashed as Jock turned back to the trainer, 'The only problem, Neilly, is that we have f*** all on the bench!'

Yes, characters all, with stories too numerous to tell, all players of a game which is not only a great leveller for every competitor, but grabs the attention of much of the world's population. And yet to think my own part in it all started with a kickabout in the back garden with my Mother's voice coming through the kitchen window ... 'Jim, you come in and do your homework, you'll never get anywhere just kicking a ball.'

DEREK JOHNSTONE

10 A BLUE DO

*Derek Johnstone shows the other side of the Old Firm coin.
Derek enjoyed a seventeen-year career with Rangers and was
known as one of the most prolific scorers of his time. Capped
by Scotland both at centre-half and centre-forward, big
Derek is now an experienced TV and radio broadcaster, and
in this chapter he looks back on some hilarious tales of his
days with the Light Blues and the Scotland international
team.*

Fans are the lifeblood of the game. They can make or break a player. They can inspire a team to unheard-of heights one day, then pressure the same side into playing like Girl Guides the next game. Get them on your side and you are halfway there. If they are against you, it's uphill all the way.

In my time at Ibrox the one player who could do no right in the eyes of the Rangers fans was Jim Denny. Jim was a helluva nice bloke with a good dry sense of humour, but to the Rangers fans he was no laughing matter. Jim, or 'Pele' as we nicknamed him, was well aware of it, too.

The crunch came one afternoon at Ibrox when we were playing Celtic. Jim was substitute that day, and midway through the first half big Jock Wallace told him to go out and have a bit of a warm-up to keep himself ready for action. Unbelievably, Jim ran towards the Celtic end and stayed for a while behind their goal. I couldn't repeat what they called him as he went through his series of stretches and sprints.

When he eventually jogged back to the dugout, big Jock was totally bemused. 'Goodness

me, Jim, why ever did you choose that end for your warm-up?' he asked. (Or words to that effect.)

Jim had the perfect reply: 'I get less stick from them.'

I have to admit, I had it fairly easy from the Rangers fans during my time there. Scoring that League Cup winner against Celtic in 1970 in only my second game obviously helped.

However, towards the end of my time at Ibrox even the memory of that header couldn't save me from the wrath of one particular gentleman.

I was playing in a midweek reserve match against St Mirren and there must have been about 60 people there, including the teams. But amongst those 60 was a spectator with the loudest voice I've ever heard at a football game. His shouts of abuse arrived on the pitch like incoming artillery . . . and he didn't like me one little bit.

To be fair to the voice in the stand, I was no longer the slimline sixteen-year-old from 1970. In fact, I was quite a bit removed from that, and my critic was quick to notice it. 'Hey

Derek Johnstone puts the other side of the Old
Firm story

Johnstone,' he roared in a voice that went right round the deserted ground. 'You've got a bigger chest than my wife.'

Heckler . . . 1   Johnstone . . . 0

So it continued, to the great amusement of my team-mates and our opponents. 'Hey Johnstone. Do you realise I gave up *Coronation Street* to watch you?'

Heckler . . . 2   Johnstone . . . 0

There was no escape from him. I was fat. I was slow. I couldn't trap a ball. I couldn't pass a ball.

Eventually when I went to take a throw-in near the dug-out, I spotted him in mid-abuse and decided to get my own back. I thought I had a great line. 'Hey you,' I shouted. 'If I'm so useless you are pretty stupid paying to watch me . . .'

Back came the reply. 'Are you kidding?' he bawled. 'I got a comp . . .'

Game, set and match to the heckler.

But one heckler didn't do so well when he decided to blast one of my players when I was manager of Partick Thistle. Once again, it was a midweek reserve game. (What is it about these matches that brings out the worst in people?) Anyway, this player of mine (he has to remain nameless for obvious reasons) was getting a really rough time from this one joker in the stand. When the team came in for their half-time chat from me, there was no consoling my man.

The player was quite honest with me. 'I'm sorry boss, but if that guy keeps that up during the second half, I'm having him at the end of the game.'

I told him not to be stupid. That if he did anything like that the club would have no option but to let him go, plus he could get into trouble with the police.

I guess my words never got through. During the second half the same fellow kept up the insults and when the final whistle blew, my man went straight up the tunnel and out the front door still in his strip and boots.

The unfortunate heckler got a quick right hook on the chops . . . and my man never played for Thistle again!

Now if only I'd thought of that one against St Mirren that night . . . !

Every football team needs a strong disciplinarian at the top and for a long time, Rangers didn't just have one – they had two of the toughest.

Big Jock Wallace was every bit as hard as people imagined. You crossed him at your peril. As well as him there was Willie Wad-

Jock Wallace, former Rangers manager, now looking after the fortunes of Colchester United in the Fourth Division

dell. Now the 'Deedle' didn't have big Jock's physique or growl, but you knew he was the gaffer. He could incinerate you with one of his stares and when he wanted to let rip with the verbals, no-one argued.

He could be great company, and still is for that matter, but generally the lads wanted to keep out of his way when they were having a few beers on a trip abroad. One memorable night, we had flown down to London, prior to flying out to Saudi Arabia first thing the next morning. John Greig was boss at that time, and all the lads were given permission to stay out quite late and have a few beers.

Well, a crowd of them came back into the hotel in the early hours of the morning and who did they see fast asleep in the foyer, but Joe Mason, who was coach of the team at the time. Josie had obviously been celebrating and was quite tired and emotional, so the lads thought they'd better help him. The hall porter provided a wheelchair and Joe, out for the count, was lifted into it and taken upstairs to Willie Waddell's room.

The lads pounded on the Deedle's door, until an angry bellow from inside signalled he was awake. Quick as a flash, the players disappeared, leaving the sleeping figure of Joe Mason to face the wrath of Willie Waddell when the door opened.

It was a very quiet Joe Mason for the rest of the trip, particularly when he learned his new nickname: 'Ironside!'

Some of the best laughs of my playing career came during trips abroad. Like the trick John Greig and I played on Tom Forsyth *en route* to Australia in the mid-seventies. Big Tam was keenly competing with Martin Buchan for the sweeper's role in the Scotland team at that time. Prior to us flying out, Buchan's manager at Manchester United, Tommy Docherty, really inflamed the situation by comparing Buchan and Forsyth as likening a thoroughbred to a carthorse.

Big Jock was none too pleased about this and had angry words with Tommy Doc about it, but the tag stuck for a while.

So there was Greigy and I stuck on this long flight to Australia and in rather a boisterous mood after a few in-flight sherries. We enlisted the help of a stewardess and headed to the back of the plane and the intercom phone.

Next minute over the plane's tannoy, came the message: 'Would Mr Tom Forsyth of the Rangers travelling party please make himself known to the cabin staff?'

'That's me, love,' said an eager big Tam, his arm up like a schoolboy asking to leave the room.

'Could you come with me, sir?' said the stewardess, leading him to the front of the plane. 'There is a telephone call for you.'

Big Tam was suitably impressed, and picked up the other intercom phone, which the stewardess handed him. 'Tom Forsyth here, who's speaking?'

'It's Jim Young here of the *Manchester Evening News*,' said John Greig in his best English accent.

'How did you get this number?' asked big Tam. He had taken the bait, and I thought Greigy and I were going to die laughing. Greigy did brilliantly to recover in time. 'Contacts, Tom. Contacts!' he said. 'But anyway, this row has flared up again. Tommy Docherty has called you a carthorse again. What do you say to that?'

'Look, I'm not saying anything,' said big Tam. 'I do my talking on the park. That's the type of man I am. But how did you say you got this number . . . ?'

Greigy couldn't continue. 'Tom,' he said. 'If you look back down the plane you'll see how we got the number.'

The big fellow looked back and all he could see were Greigy and I holding on to the phone and howling with laughter.

The big fellow was not a happy man, and he

spent the rest of that holiday getting his revenge . . . and that was painful. There was nothing subtle about big Tam's revenge. If he caught you alone in a lift, he knocked lumps out of you in the privacy of the elevator.

Well, that was a month-long tour and by the end of it, I was climbing twelve flights of stairs rather than risk a meeting with him. (PS   If he was a carthorse, I wish we'd had ten more of them.)

Once during that same Australian trip the laugh was on John Greig in one memorable incident. As part of the tour we had to play the Australian national XI in a variety of venues throughout the country and towards the end

of the trip we had to face them yet again in Perth.

We hadn't lost to them, but in this particular game we were losing 1–0 with a few minutes to go and were pushing hard for the equaliser. Greigy went on a great run and got right through their defence with only the keeper to beat. But as he lifted his leg to shoot, their big centre-half clipped his ankle to send Greigy flying. In fact, he nearly rolled the length of the pitch – the size of him.

When he got up, he wasn't a happy man and

Tom Forsyth playing the sweeper's role for Scotland *v* Argentina

he chased after the big Aussie with a crowd of us trying to stop him before he did anything silly.

Too late . . . he reached the Aussie before we could, grabbed him by the throat and said viciously, 'See you, son, your mark's card!'

I think the Australian must have thought it was some kind of Gaelic curse, because he looked puzzled, but the rest of us just dissolved at Greigy's slip of the tongue, which became the team's catchphrase for quite a while.

It's not just players and punters who can come up with the good lines. Referees in my time could be quick to bring you down a peg. Like Kenny Hope did to me at Pittodrie one day. We were playing Aberdeen in the second leg of a League Cup tie and had gone up there with a 2–0 lead. They clawed that back and with a few minutes to go, the teams were tied 2–2 on aggregate and it was all to play for.

Then Colin Jackson brought one of their men down. To this day I still say it was outside the area, but the referee didn't agree. He gave a penalty. They scored and I was raging . . . 'Kenny, that was never a **** penalty,' I screamed at him. He pulled me aside. 'Big man,' he said, 'read about it in tomorrow's papers.'

Although I was angry at the time, I respect Kenny Hope for the way he handled that situation. I should have been off the park for what I'd said, but he realised the passion in the game and had tried to cool the situation with a bit of patter.

I don't know if today's breed of referee would handle the situation as well. From what I see and hear I think there is now a much bigger gap between officials and players than there was in my day, and I think it is bad for the game.

But one final thought, Mr Hope. I still don't think it was a **** penalty!

Colin Jackson, the man at the centre of that Aberdeen penalty incident, was one of the great characters during my Rangers days. Bomber, as we called him, was the first yuppie – fifteen years before the world heard of them.

He often wore the most outrageous gear which had the dressing room totally bemused. One day he rolled up to Ibrox wearing a pair of cowboy boots, spurs and all. The lads slagged them mercilessly, but Bomber quietly ignored all the stick. They were his pride and joy.

Off we went training, but Colin Stein, always a joker, had to leave the session early when he tweaked a hamstring. When we got back to the dressing room, Steiny was already dressed and there was a mischievous gleam in his eye, but we didn't know why until Bomber started to get dressed.

He got all his gear on, slipped on his socks, stepped into his cowboy boots and didn't move an inch. Colin Stein had nailed them to the floor.

Bomber wasn't pleased. Great six-inch nails driven through his boots! But even he had to laugh when the whole dressing room started singing 'These Boots Ain't Made for Walking.'

Scotland striker Ally McCoist is the present clown prince of Ibrox. He is quick-witted with a great sense of humour and usually comes off best when trading insults.

Big Peter McCloy couldn't match Ally verbally, but he had his own way of dealing with the problem. This particular day Ally was hitting the big fellow with a stream of one-liners. All Peter was doing was keeping count. 'That's one, two, three so far,' said Peter. 'Any more, Ally?'

McCoist continued to come up with the insults. Eventually Peter's count had risen to 20. 'That's enough,' he said, and left the dressing room.

Two minutes later, he was back wearing

the boxing gloves that were kept by the punchbag in the weights room. 'All right, McCoist,' he said. 'Your time's up. You are going to get one thump for every bit of cheek I've had to take.'

And he set about Ally, counting as he did it. 'That's one ... two ... three ... four,' he counted off, each number proceeded by a thump and a squeal of pain from McCoist.

It was hilarious to watch, particularly when Ally threw in a bit more cheek during the onslaught and Peter simply said, 'Very foolish, Coisty, you're getting another one for that.' Whack!

It became a standard dressing-room joke that Peter always donned the gloves when Ally gave him cheek. No-one liked it better than McCoist, except for a couple of times when Peter's playful slaps got a little too rough.

We all joined in the fun. I remember walking back from the Albion training ground with Ally after a practice match, and Ally was telling me a few of the lines he was going to say to Peter in the dressing room. As soon as we got into Ibrox I went straight to the weights room, picked up the gloves and headed for the dressing room. McCoist hadn't

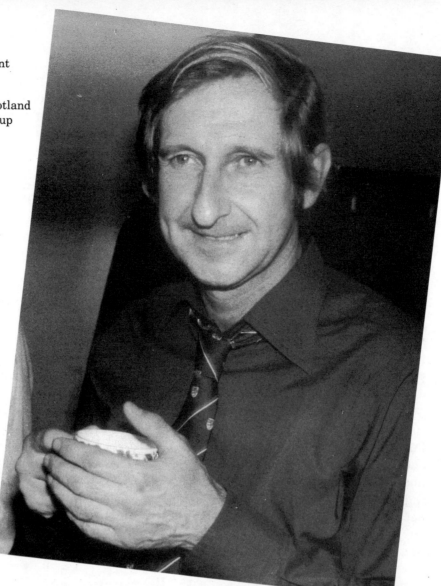

Left: Ally McCoist – present clown prince at Ibrox

Right: Ally MacLeod – Scotland team boss in the World Cup Finals, Argentina, 1978

opened his mouth yet, but I just handed the gloves to Big Peter.

'You are going to need them, big fellow,' I said. 'You should hear the things McCoist was saying about you coming back from the Albion.'

'Is that right?' said big Peter, donning the gloves and glaring at Ally. 'Come here, you.' Whack! Whack! Whack!

When football teams are staying in hotels, managers employ all sorts of spies to make sure their curfews are enforced. Barmen, porters and reception clerks are all briefed to keep the boss posted if any player breaks any of the rules.

It's usually an unbeatable system, and Ally MacLeod went one better when he was Scotland boss in the World Cup in Argentina in 1978. The Scotland party had just arrived at Cordoba, and as soon as we had dumped our bags in our rooms a group of us went for a walk through the hotel grounds to get a look at what was to be our home for quite a while.

We had the hotel to ourselves and had been told not to leave the grounds, but when we got to one particular boundary wall, what did we see over the wall but a casino cum nightclub. It seemed so inviting, and anyway, what harm would having a look do?

As we put a hand on the wall to vault it, I stopped stock still. Three trees back from the wall had started to move towards us. This was the Argentinian security service, and boy were they thorough. I can still visualise the slits in the trees for them to see out of, and this voice coming out from behind the slit saying, 'Pleeze, pleeze, you must go back!'

It was the last time we ever tested that security again . . . mind you, now I know how Macbeth felt!

I scored a lot of goals with my head, and people seem to remember that particular aspect of my game, more than anything else! But I had a fair dig with either foot, as Scotland trainer Hugh Allan found out to his cost one day. I was in a Scotland Under-21 squad and we were based in Stonehaven before playing England in a match at Pittodrie. We went out for some light training at Stonehaven one day, and I remember it was absolutely freezing. All the brass monkeys in the town were wearing thermal vests.

As usual, the training session opened with us all having some shooting practice and we were blasting in shots from all angles. It was one way to get a bit warmer.

Then Hugh decided we had better do a bit more strenuous work, so he called for the balls to be returned to him. As the lads lobbed the balls back to Hugh, one came my way and I decided to have one last dig at goal, and I whacked this thing as hard as I could.

Unfortunately for me, and for Hugh, I mis-kicked it and it flew off my foot at right angles and hit Hugh full in the face. Thump! Right on the kisser . . . I'm sure you could see the name Mitre stamped on his forehead.

Now Hugh is a hardy wee man, and he had to be that day. It must have been sore, but I remember he just shook his head once and got on with the rest of the training session. He didn't say one word to me, but deep down he must have been angry and it showed when he read out the teams for the practice matches. 'On one side, we'll have Jim, Dave, Tommy, Tony, Ian, Eddie and Frank,' said Hugh, reading off a bit of paper. 'Against Alan, Jimmy, Stuart, Pat, Kenny, Iain and JOHNSTONE!'

I was the only one that didn't get called by my first name.